Praise for *Unbreakable Alliances*

"Working with countless jurors and witnesses, I've often wondered, *What is the key to evaluating them effectively in such a high-stakes setting?* Robin Dreeke's new book *Unbreakable Alliances*, simply put? Amazing!"
—Nancy Grace, Host, *Crime Stories with Nancy Grace*

"This is Robin Dreeke's best book. Factual, useful, and full of wisdom and proven techniques that will improve your skill set. I love this book, and the knowledge and experience Robin shares is priceless."
—Joe Navarro, International Bestselling Author, *Be Exceptional*

"In our ever-changing world, where uncertainty looms, certain skills become the bedrock of success. Enter *Unbreakable Alliances*: equipping you with the essential tools to succeed—no matter what. These are the skills that determine success. As AI continues to shape our reality and politics evolve, Robin imparts wisdom that transcends mere knowledge. Consider this book not just a companion, but a mentor—a trusted ally on your journey toward mastery."
—Chase Hughes, #1 Bestselling Author, *The Behavior Ops Manual*, and CEO, Applied Behavior Research

"In *Unbreakable Alliances*, Robin reveals the secrets he learned from his experiences as an FBI behavioral analyst. This book is a must-read for people who want to learn how to create and maintain trust relationships and alliances. Robin provides practical examples that illustrate his step-by-step method to develop trusting relationships and alliances."
—Dr. Jack Schafer, Author, *The Like Switch*, and retired FBI Agent

"*Unbreakable Alliances* is a groundbreaking book that highlights the paramount importance of alliances and healthy relationships in all areas of life. With its unique focus on cultivating powerful and lasting connections, the book offers unparalleled insights and practical techniques that set it apart from any other book, making it an essential read for individuals seeking to thrive in their personal and professional endeavors. I especially enjoyed and resonated with the book's insights about the crucial importance of nonverbal communication and emotional intelligence in building rapport and trust, exercising nonjudgmental listening and empathy, and developing unbreakable alliances. I know readers will be as inspired as I was after reading this book!"

—Dr. David Matsumoto, Director, Humintell, and Professor
of Psychology, San Francisco State University

"Prepare to be empowered and inspired! In Robin's groundbreaking book, readers are taken on a transformative journey, unlocking the secrets to cultivating indispensable alliances. With actionable insights and real-world strategies, Robin reveals the keys to forging powerful connections that propel both personal and professional success. A must-read for anyone looking to master the art of building and maintaining meaningful relationships."

—Jana Monroe, Author, *Hearts of Darkness*

"As a body language and behavior analyst, I found Robin's new book invaluable for enhancing my work. It brilliantly bridges the gap between espionage techniques and everyday personal skills. I can't recommend it enough for anyone looking to deepen their understanding of human behavior and forge lasting relationships."

—Scott Rouse, Body Language Expert and Behavior Analyst

"Dreeke shares FBI worldwide expertise to empower readers in forging powerful alliances. From leveraging allies to mastering trust and communication, each principle is essential for navigating modern business."

—Mark Bowden, Communication Advisor to G7 Leaders

"Robin is a rare convergence of razor-sharp skills gained from decades of investigation, a continuing love of people, and the ability to teach you what he knows. Reading this book will change your relationships and life."

—Greg Hartley, Body Language and Human Behavior Expert

UNBREAKABLE
ALLIANCES

Also by Robin Dreeke

It's Not All About Me: The Top Ten Techniques
for Building Quick Rapport with Anyone

The Code of Trust: An American Counterintelligence
Expert's Five Rules to Lead and Succeed

Sizing People Up: A Veteran FBI Agent's User
Manual for Behavior Prediction

UNBREAKABLE ALLIANCES

A Spy Recruiter's Authoritative Guide to Cultivating Powerful and Lasting Connections

ROBIN DREEKE

Matt Holt Books
An Imprint of BenBella Books, Inc.
Dallas, TX

Matt Holt is an imprint of BenBella Books, Inc.
10440 N. Central Expressway, Suite 800
Dallas, TX 75231
benbellabooks.com
Send feedback to feedback@benbellabooks.com.

BenBella and *Matt Holt* are federally registered trademarks.

Printed in the United States of America
10 9 8 7 6 5 4 3 2 1

Library of Congress Control Number: 2024011520
ISBN 978-1-63774-592-2 (hardcover)
ISBN 978-1-63774-593-9 (electronic)

Copyediting by James Fraleigh
Proofreading by Denise Pangia and Cape Cod Compositors, Inc.
Indexing by WordCo Indexing Services, Inc.
Text design and composition by Aaron Edmiston
Cover design by Brigid Pearson
Printed by Lake Book Manufacturing

Special discounts for bulk sales are available.
Please contact bulkorders@benbellabooks.com.

Dedicated to my greatest Unbreakable Allies:
My wife, Kim, my daughter, Katelyn, and my son, Kevin

CONTENTS

INTRODUCTION

Welcome to the captivating world of alliances and the art of creating unbreakable allies. As you delve into the pages of *Unbreakable Alliances*, prepare yourself for a thought-provoking exploration of personal and professional growth as you've never experienced it. I will share these skills and techniques with you using examples from life, business, and my time in the Federal Bureau of Investigation leading the Counterintelligence Division's Behavioral Analysis Program. The anecdotes used throughout the book are fictional but based on my career of working these types of cases with the allies mentioned throughout.

But this book is not a mere collection of theories and concepts. It is a reference and mastery workbook designed to empower you to take action and achieve tangible results. From recognizing the importance of alliances to cultivating active listening, empathy, and curiosity, these actions will set you on the path to building unbreakable alliances.

In chapter one, "FOCUS: The Power of Allies," I will take you on a thrilling journey through a high-stakes spy case to reveal the immense power of alliances. I will introduce the four keys to effective communication, which will serve as a powerful anchor throughout the book. I will help you overcome skepticism and fear as we take that leap of faith, mastering conflict resolution and finding common ground through problem solving. Prepare to build trust through your own behavioral skills and to become the lighthouse that guides others toward success. This chapter will reveal the solution to life's challenges that lies beyond the locked door of self-doubt, waiting to be discovered through relationships and alliances.

In chapter two, "TRUST: Building It, Keeping It," we will explore the transformative power of rapport and trust in business leadership. Through captivating anecdotes and effective techniques, you will gain the insights needed to establish genuine connections with others, building successful alliances and easing doubts. Prepare to harness the power of active listening, nonverbal cues, and credibility as you build trust brick by brick. You will learn how to inspire allies, embrace diversity, and craft compelling narratives that ignite inspiration.

Chapter three, "COMMUNICATE: The Golden Key to Success," will equip you with the tools to communicate with impact and enhance your alliances. Together, we will dig deeper still into the power of empathy, learning to tailor communication styles to others and leverage nonverbal cues for deeper understanding. Prepare to navigate language barriers and master the art of virtual communication. The realm of EQ will unfold, enhancing your ability to connect and influence.

In chapter four, "INSPIRE: Moving Beyond Influence and Persuasion," we will embark on a journey to inspire others and forge unbreakable alliances. I will show you how to perceive the nuances that distinguish influence, persuasion, and inspiration as you apply the keys to communication to inspire those around us. You will learn to embrace diversity and inclusion while tailoring your approach to each individual. Prepare to craft compelling narratives that captivate hearts and minds as you leave a lasting impact.

Chapter five, "OWN IT: Resolving Conflicts Through Your Actions," will guide you through the labyrinth of conflicts within alliances. You will learn to understand different viewpoints, conquer the pitfalls of ego, and master emotions during conflicts. Prepare to uncover the laws of human nature, enhance your deception-detection skills, and discover the dichotomy of freedom and discipline. By cultivating self-leadership, and embracing constructive feedback and respectful disagreement, you will foster stronger alliances.

In chapter six, "CONTEXT: The Recipe for Acceptance and Understanding," we will explore the power of understanding and embracing diversity in alliances. Prepare to unlock the importance of being present, welcoming differences, and overcoming communication barriers. You will unleash the power of deep curiosity, innovation, and psychological safety. Embrace the path to unbreakable alliances through deep context understanding.

Chapter seven, "BUILD: The Power of Long-Term Alliances," will equip you with the strategies to nurture and expand your alliances over time. We will build communication channels, establish trust and credibility, and conquer the pitfalls of ego. With these skills, you will adapt and thrive in your alliances, address concerns and conflicts, and express gratitude and appreciation, thus ensuring that your alliances will endure.

Last, chapter eight, "MASTERY: Moving Beyond Natural Talent," will set you on a journey of self-awareness and self-mastery. You will discover the behavior keys to mastery, strike the delicate balance between authenticity and boundaries, and cultivate self-mastery for alliance creation.

In addition, each chapter is accompanied by ten actions that will enable you to apply what you learn in your own life and work. The book ends with a list of practical mastery exercises for long-term success, which will solidify your learning and propel your alliance-building skills to new heights.

Unbreakable Alliances is not just a book; it is a transformative experience. Prepare to unlock the immense power of alliances, build unbreakable relationships, and achieve unparalleled success in your personal and professional lives. The journey starts now, and I am here to guide you every step of the way. Together, we will revolutionize the way you approach alliances and create a legacy of enduring success.

1

FOCUS

The Power of Allies

When we are no longer able to change a situation,
we are challenged to change ourselves.
—Viktor Frankl

Black Viper

Imagine a high-stakes international spy case, where the fate of nations hangs in the balance. As a seasoned intelligence officer, I found myself thrust into the heart of such a mission, one that would test the limits of my skills and the power of my alliances.

The mission involved infiltrating a shadowy intelligence organization I'll call Black Viper. They had been wreaking havoc across the globe, carrying out cyberattacks and destabilizing governments. It was clear that their reach and influence extended far beyond what any single agency could handle.

Recognizing the need for a united front, I began forging alliances with intelligence agencies worldwide. Each had their own expertise and resources that, when combined, would create an unstoppable force against Black Viper.

One of my key alliances was with a British agent I'll call Alex. He had been tracking Black Viper for months and had invaluable intelligence on their inner workings. We shared a common goal and a burning desire to end the organization's reign of terror.

Together, Alex and I formed a tight-knit duo, pooling our knowledge, skills, and resources. We worked tirelessly, coordinating surveillance operations, analyzing intercepted communications, and gathering evidence. Our alliance allowed us to navigate the murky world of international espionage, blending our unique approaches and perspectives to stay one step ahead of Black Viper's elusive leaders.

But our alliance didn't stop with just the two of us. We enlisted the support of agents from Australia, France, and other countries' intelligence agencies from across the globe. Together, we were a formidable network that spanned continents and time zones, united in our mission to bring down Black Viper.

As the operation unfolded, we faced countless obstacles and near-impossible challenges. But the power of our alliances propelled us forward. The trust we had built, the shared resources, and the combined expertise allowed us to outmaneuver Black Viper at every turn.

In the end, our alliances proved key to our success. Black Viper was dismantled, their leadership captured, and their operations thwarted. It was a resounding victory, not just for our agencies, but for the safety and security of the world.

Though a typical spy case, it taught me a valuable lesson: in the world of international espionage, alliances are not just an option—they are a necessity. By leveraging multiple agencies' strengths and resources, we were able to achieve what any single agency would have found impossible.

Throughout *Unbreakable Alliances*, I will share the principles and techniques I used to build this coalition, which I have honed throughout my career as an international spy recruiter. We will explore the transformative power of alliances and how they can bring success in our careers and lives. I have spent my life studying human behavior and the art of building strong relationships. Through my experiences as an FBI agent, I have come to understand the vital role that alliances play in our journey toward success. Whether you are an intelligence operative, a business leader, or simply someone navigating complex relationships, this book will guide you toward success through the power of alliances.

But what exactly do we mean by "alliances"? Put simply, alliances are the relationships we forge with others that enable us to navigate the complexities of life. As social creatures, we are wired for connection. From the moment we are born, our survival depends on the alliances we form with our parents or caregivers. This initial bond of trust provides us with a sense of safety and the freedom to explore the world around us.

As we grow, alliances become the foundation on which we build our lives. We rely on neighbors, friends, and family to support us through challenges and share in our triumphs. These alliances are not just important for our emotional well-being; they also have a profound impact on our brain chemistry. Whether we are introverts or extroverts, the quality of our relationships directly affects our mental health.

In our post-pandemic world, we have witnessed the devastating consequences of isolation. The lack of alliances has taken a toll on people's mental health worldwide. We clearly need alliances to thrive in our personal lives, but their importance extends far beyond that.

In the realm of business, alliances are the lifeblood of success. The modern business landscape is fraught with complexity, dueling priorities, and ever-evolving challenges. As individuals and in our organizations, we cannot hope to innovate and overcome these hurdles without the power of alliances. By allying with those who share our goals, priorities, and aspirations, we gain access to a wealth of resources and expertise. These alliances become the driving force behind our ability to solve problems and achieve our objectives.

So, what exactly defines an alliance? In my view, an alliance is a relationship where individuals, groups, or organizations are aware of each other's goals, needs, and pain points. They are willing to provide resources and support to one another, both short and long term. The highest level of alliances goes beyond mere awareness; here, people are proactive in offering assistance and resources to ensure mutual success.

However, what if I told you that the key to unlocking that door lies not in your own hands alone, but in the power of alliances? By embracing the concept of alliances and understanding their true potential, we can open up a world of possibilities and solutions that were previously out of reach. In this next section, we will delve deeper into how alliances can be vital for overcoming challenges and finding the solutions we seek.

Unlocking the Power of Alliances:
The Solution Lies Beyond the Locked Door

Have you ever found yourself facing a seemingly insurmountable challenge or problem and then searched desperately for a solution? It's as though you're pounding on the door right in front of you, hoping that it will magically open and reveal the answer. But as you continue to beat on that metaphorical door, your frustration builds because it remains locked, keeping the solution hidden from you.

We've all been there, haven't we? It's a common experience, relatable to us all. The truth is, sometimes the solution we seek isn't found by pounding on that locked door. Instead, it lies in unlocking the door through the power of alliances and the people around us.

Think about it. When we take a step back, relax, and sensitize our allies to the challenge and pain we are facing, something magical happens. Suddenly, our reliance on others and the healthy relationships we have formed combine to bring forth innovative solutions to complex ideas. It's as if the locked door effortlessly swings open, revealing the answers we were desperately seeking.

This is the true power and importance of having alliances. They provide us with fresh perspectives, diverse expertise, and a support system that can help us overcome even the most daunting obstacles. When we embrace the value of alliances, we tap into a wealth of knowledge and experience that can propel us toward success.

But building alliances isn't always easy. One of the biggest challenges people face is trust. Trust is the bedrock of any successful alliance; without it, our ability to form meaningful connections has no foundation. When we are plagued by fear and insecurity, we find it difficult to trust others, which hinders our progress.

To overcome this challenge, it is essential for us to understand the behaviors of trust. In forging alliances, we must demonstrate through our own actions that we are trustworthy. Yet we must also develop the ability to recognize trustworthy behaviors in others. Assessing trustworthiness is not just about feelings; it's also about observing the behaviors that create a safe environment for collaboration. We will explore advanced behavioral techniques and strategies that will help you overcome the challenges of building alliances. By understanding the cognitive, thoughtful behaviors behind trust, you can tap the power of alliances and create unbreakable bonds that lead to success.

So, the next time you find yourself pounding on that locked door, take a step back, reach out to your alliances, and watch as the solution effortlessly reveals itself. Remember, the key to unlocking success lies in the power of alliances.

Building Trust Through Behavior Skills

In my experience, the secret of creating successful alliances lies in the behaviors we demonstrate. But before we can lead others, we must first learn to lead ourselves. It all starts with trust, and that begins with open, honest communication. We must be transparent and vulnerable while demonstrating our competence.

Let's break it down further. Open and honest communication is crucial because it makes others feel safe. We need to be straightforward; if we cannot share certain information because of rules or policies, it's important to be up front about this and explain the reason behind it. This level of transparency builds trust and shows that we respect the other person's intelligence.

Transparency goes hand in hand with open communication. People are observant and perceptive, so it's essential to give them credit for doing their due diligence. By sharing information, we validate what they already know and ensure that our actions align with what we say. This concept is similar to the old Russian expression, "Trust but verify." It's not about being skeptical or cynical; rather, we spot-check occasionally to ensure that the transparency we're receiving is genuine.

Next comes vulnerability, which many find challenging. People often fear being taken advantage of when they show their vulnerabilities. However, truly self-assured individuals do not hide their weaknesses. Instead, they openly share what they excel at and how they mitigate their shortcomings. By embracing vulnerability, we foster a sense of trust because it shows that we are willing to share even potentially detrimental information. This behavior increases the likelihood of accurate, transparent, and honest communication.

But vulnerability alone is not enough. We must also back it up with reliability and competence. If we claim to be capable of something, we must deliver on that promise. It's better to undersell our capabilities and overperform than to oversell and underperform. By consistently proving our reliability, we maintain credibility and deepen trust.

All of these behaviors revolve around trust. Trust is the foundation upon which alliances are built. When we center our focus on others, demonstrating open communication, transparency, vulnerability, and competence, we create a reservoir of goodwill. This reservoir never drains as long as we continue to fill it by prioritizing the needs and interests of others. And when the time comes, we can make withdrawals from that reservoir, knowing that the trust we've built will support us.

Remember, creating allies is about keeping the focus off of ourselves and placing it on the other person or organization. It's about finding the balance between self and others, ensuring that trust is maintained. It's easy to take these skills for granted, but they are the guiding principles that will lead us to success in forging unbreakable alliances.

Becoming the Lighthouse

In this fast-paced, interconnected world, it is crucial for individuals to recognize the true value of alliances and understand the long-term benefits they can bring. But what exactly is their value? How can they transform our lives and propel us to success? These questions, although seemingly simple, hold profound significance that often goes unnoticed in our daily lives.

Let me ask you this: What is the most valuable asset you possess? Is it your wealth? Your possessions? Your network? While these factors may contribute to your success, there is something far more powerful and intangible that sets you apart from the rest: your reputation.

Yes, your reputation is the key to unlocking the doors of opportunity and forging unbreakable alliances. It is what defines you in the eyes of others, whether you are known as someone who is competent, giving, caring, and trustworthy, or someone who remains neutral and unknown. The importance of alliances lies in the word-of-mouth recommendations that stem from a strong reputation. Your brand, your image, your essence—they all go a long way in shaping the trajectory of your success.

Think about it. Some individuals and organizations achieve remarkable success without the aid of traditional big-budget marketing teams or sales strategies. They rely heavily on their reputation and the alliances they have cultivated along their journey. These are the individuals who truly understand the power of alliances and the enduring benefits they bring. They are the ones who experience organic success—success that grows naturally and effortlessly.

So, how does this organic success come about? It all boils down to one fundamental question: Are you the person in someone's life who consistently solves problems, offers resources proactively, and is always available to provide guidance? Sometimes that support may be in the form of a listening ear. Are you the lighthouse that offers a safe harbor for those in need?

When you become this go-to person, the trusted ally, the reliable source of wisdom and support, your reputation spreads like wildfire. You become the beacon of hope that people turn to when they face insurmountable challenges or seemingly impossible situations. Your name is whispered in the corridors of opportunity, and your alliances become your greatest asset.

Just imagine the possibilities. By cultivating and nurturing lasting alliances, you not only enhance your own success but also become a catalyst for the success of others. Your influence ripples through the interconnected web of relationships, creating a powerful network of allies who are united by a common purpose: to uplift and empower one another.

But remember, becoming the lighthouse requires unwavering commitment and dedication. It demands that you consistently offer your expertise, time, and resources to those who seek your guidance. It is a responsibility that should not be taken lightly, for the impact you have on others can shape their destinies and leave a lasting legacy.

As we embark on this journey together, let us further explore the world of alliances and discover the expert techniques that will enable us to create unbreakable bonds. Let us challenge ourselves to think critically, to reflect upon our own reputations, and to embrace the power of alliances with open hearts and open minds.

Are you ready to become the lighthouse that guides others toward success?

Unlocking the Power of Communication: The Four Keys to Building Strong Alliances

In my early days in the Marine Corps, I found myself at the bottom of the rankings. I was rated last out of all the second lieutenants in my squadron. Determined to improve, I approached my unit's major and asked him for guidance. I took ownership of my failure, understanding that placing blame wouldn't get me anywhere, then asked, "What am I doing wrong?"

He looked at me and said, "You just need to be a better leader."

It sounded simple, but I needed more guidance. "How do I become a better leader?"

He smiled and said, "That's easy. Make it about everyone else but yourself."

With the major's enigmatic response echoing in my mind, I began a quest to unravel the secrets of effective communication, and soon uncovered four keys to unlocking this skill. The first key is *seeking the thoughts and opinions of others instead of solely focusing on sharing my own*. It dawned on me that genuine listening and valuing the input of those around me were paramount. In my pursuit of finding allies who truly understood and respected my thoughts and opinions, I began to prioritize individuals who possessed the same qualities, which cultivated a mutual exchange of ideas.

The second key is *speaking in terms of others' priorities, challenges, and pain points instead of your own*. It's about empathizing and showing genuine interest in the concerns of those you want to ally with. I pay attention to whether potential allies talk in terms of my priorities and challenges.

The third key is *practicing nonjudgmental curiosity*—being open minded and validating others' choices and decisions, both professionally and personally. I appreciate when potential allies show curiosity and refrain from passing judgment.

Last, the fourth key is *empowering others with choices*. Giving someone a choice makes them feel safe and valued. When assessing potential allies, I look for individuals who empower me with choices, showing that they trust and respect my judgment.

By actively listening to your team members and valuing their input, you create an environment that empowers them with choices. As you open up the floor for discussion and encourage different perspectives, you demonstrate trust and respect for their judgment. This creates a sense of safety while encouraging collaboration and innovation. Just as you appreciate when others empower you with choices, it is equally important to empower those around you.

Example: Seeking Thoughts and Opinions

Imagine you're meeting with your team, discussing a crucial project. As the leader, you have your own ideas and thoughts about how things should be done. However, you remember the first key to communication: seeking the thoughts and opinions of others.

Instead of immediately sharing your own ideas, you turn to your team members and ask, "What are your thoughts on this project? How do you think we should approach it?" You genuinely listen to their responses, encouraging them to express their ideas freely.

One team member, Sarah, raises a valid point that you hadn't considered before. Her suggestion aligns with the priorities and goals of the project, and you appreciate her fresh perspective. By seeking her thoughts and opinions, you make her feel valued while also benefiting from her insights.

In this scenario, you demonstrate the first key to communication by actively seeking the thoughts and opinions of others. This approach sounds and is simple, but is commonly overlooked. It nurtures collaboration, encourages diverse perspectives, and ultimately leads to better decision making and stronger alliances within your team.

Example: Speaking in Terms of Others' Priorities, Challenges, and Pain Points

Let's say you're attending a networking event where you hope to find potential allies for your business. As you strike up conversations with different individuals, you remember the second key to communication: speaking in terms of others' priorities, challenges, and pain points.

You meet someone named Jordan, who runs a small marketing agency. Instead of immediately talking about your own business and its achievements, you ask Jordan questions about their work.

You inquire about the challenges they face in the industry, the priorities they have for their clients, and the pain points they regularly encounter.

As Jordan shares their experiences and concerns, you actively listen and empathize with their situation. You respond by discussing how your business has tackled similar challenges in the past and how you prioritize meeting clients' needs effectively. By tailoring your conversation to address their priorities, challenges, and pain points, you establish a connection based on shared experiences and goals.

In this encounter, you exemplify the second key to communication by speaking in terms of Jordan's priorities, challenges, and pain points. By showing genuine interest in their concerns, you build rapport, demonstrate empathy, and lay the foundation for a potential alliance.

Example: Practicing Nonjudgmental Curiosity

Imagine you're attending a conference, and during a networking session, you come across a fellow attendee named Mark. As you begin chatting, you remember the third key to communication: practicing nonjudgmental curiosity.

As Mark shares details about his business venture, you resist the urge to make assumptions or pass judgment based on your preconceived notions. Instead, you maintain an open mind and ask questions to understand his perspective better.

Mark mentions a unique approach he's taken in his industry, which initially surprises you. Instead of dismissing it or expressing skepticism, you respond with genuine curiosity. You ask him to elaborate on his strategy, wanting to understand the reasoning behind it and the results he's achieved.

By approaching the conversation with nonjudgmental curiosity, you create a safe space for Mark to share his ideas and experiences openly. Your genuine interest in his choices and willingness to learn from him foster a positive and respectful dialogue. As a result, Mark feels validated, and you engage in a meaningful exchange of ideas.

In this scenario, you embody the third key to communication by practicing nonjudgmental curiosity. By letting go of biases and embracing a genuine desire to learn from others, you create an environment conducive to building strong alliances based on mutual respect and understanding.

Example: Empowering Others with Choices

Let's say you're working on a collaborative project with a team of colleagues. As the project leader, you understand the importance of empowering others with choices, which reminds you of the fourth key to communication.

During a team meeting, you present a challenge that needs to be addressed. Instead of dictating a specific solution or approach, you turn to your team and say, "We have a few options to consider. What do you think would be the best course of action?"

By giving your team members the freedom to choose and contribute to the decision-making process, you empower them to take ownership of their ideas and feel more engaged in the project. Each team member offers their perspective, discussing the pros and cons of different approaches.

As the discussion unfolds, you actively listen to their suggestions, encouraging them to explore their ideas further. Eventually, the team collectively decides on a course of action that everyone feels confident about because they had a say in the decision-making process.

In this example, you demonstrate the fourth key to communication by empowering others with choices. By giving your team members a sense of autonomy and involving them in decision making, you cultivate a collaborative environment while building trust and strengthening the alliance within your team.

But what about biases and preconceived notions? How can we overcome them and cultivate open-mindedness toward potential allies? The answer lies in curiosity. We must let go of our assumptions and be present in our interactions.

We should always remember that everyone is seeking a healthy and prosperous life for themselves and their loved ones. Understanding this fundamental desire helps us let go of biases and realize that others' actions and choices are driven by what they believe is in their best interest.

Brené Brown once said, "If you don't understand someone, get closer."[1] This quote resonates with me because it reminds us to approach others with genuine curiosity. It is important to remember that we must first take off our own shoes before we can truly walk in someone else's.

Let go of your biases, be curious, and engage with potential allies with an open mind. Building strong alliances is about making it about others, understanding their perspectives, and empowering them with choices. By embracing these principles, you can create unbreakable alliances and achieve success in any endeavor.

The First Move: A Leap of Faith

In the world of building alliances, skepticism and fear are often formidable obstacles. Overcoming these initial barriers requires a strategic approach that embraces the power of trust and vulnerability. As Simon Sinek aptly suggests, the best organizations invest in failure, understanding that taking the first step in building trust may not always yield immediate success.[2]

It is essential to simplify the process by making the first move. Demonstrating your trust and willingness to take a calculated risk sends a powerful message to potential allies. However, you must prepare for the possibility that things may not go as planned. Recognizing the potential risks and rewards and being prepared to navigate the unexpected are crucial aspects of forging unbreakable alliances.

The Paradox of Patience

Building trust in a world of skepticism requires a unique blend of patience and persistence. When individuals or groups enter into a new relationship or alliance with you, they may be understandably skeptical. They may question your true intentions and wonder if there are hidden agendas at play. The only way to overcome these doubts is through patience, time, and consistently aligning your words, actions, and deeds.

Patience allows you to withstand others' initial doubts and reservations, giving them the space and time to witness the congruence between what you say and what you do. Through this congruence, trust begins to take root and grow. As challenging as it may be, practicing patience is a vital component of building unbreakable alliances.

Vulnerability as a Catalyst for Trust

Trust and vulnerability are inextricably linked. The ability to be vulnerable and show your true intentions is a powerful catalyst for building trust. In a world that often values strength and invulnerability, embracing vulnerability can feel counterintuitive. However, it is in moments of vulnerability that we open ourselves up to genuine connections and create opportunities for trust to flourish.

By demonstrating authenticity and transparency, you create an environment where others feel safe and valued. Willingly exposing your vulnerabilities encourages others to do the same, fostering a deeper level of trust and understanding. Embracing vulnerability is not a sign of weakness, but rather a testament to your strength as a leader.

By challenging your thinking, reflecting on your own behaviors, and embracing the transformative power of trust and vulnerability, you will unlock the secrets to creating unbreakable alliances. Are you ready to take the first step and embrace the journey that lies ahead?

Managing Conflicts and Finding Common Ground: The Power of Problem Solving

Let me tell you a little story about something I like to call the "what, who, how, and why" problem-solving approach. It's like having a secret weapon in your arsenal when conflicts arise in alliances.

Once, in a small town, there was a group of individuals who had formed an alliance to accomplish a shared goal. They were passionate, talented, and driven, but as with any group, conflicts appeared.

Each member had their own ideas, skills, and experiences, which sometimes led to clashes and differences of opinion.

One day, during a particularly heated discussion, they realized that they were all approaching the problem from different angles. They were focusing on the "what, how, and who" aspects of the challenge, but they had forgotten the most important piece of the puzzle—the "why."

Taking a step back, they realized that they had lost sight of the overarching purpose and objective of their alliance. They had forgotten to align their efforts toward a common outcome, as if they were all trying to reach the same destination via different paths.

With this realization, they reframed their approach. They took the time to establish what they were truly seeking to accomplish—their shared mission. By doing so, they found common ground and a renewed sense of purpose.

As they continued to work together, conflicts still arose, but now they had a powerful tool to manage them. Whenever disagreements surfaced, they would remind themselves of their shared outcome and stay open to different perspectives. They understood that each member brought unique skills, tools, techniques, and experiences to the table, and that diversity could be harnessed for creative problem solving.

This anecdote illustrates the importance of having a clear "why" in an alliance. It reminds us that conflicts and friction points are natural and can actually be opportunities for growth. By maintaining trust and a reservoir of goodwill, by routinely being transparent and maintaining conscious, thoughtful processes, we can navigate these conflicts and find common ground.

By applying this problem-solving approach, you can ensure that conflicting interests do not derail your alliance. Remember, alliances are about balance, maintaining dichotomies, and establishing milestones and guideposts. They are not about one party taking more than they give. As long as you nurture a healthy and open relationship, you will unlock the true potential of your alliance.

The next time conflicts arise in your alliances, remember the power of the "what, who, how, and why" approach. Embrace diversity, maintain trust, and keep your eyes on the shared outcome. With these principles in mind, you will be well equipped to navigate the complexities of alliance management and achieve unbreakable success.

Throughout this book, I will share the guiding principles and expert techniques that will empower you to create unbreakable alliances. Drawing from my experiences in the FBI and my deep understanding of human behavior, I will provide you with the tools and strategies to cultivate meaningful connections and harness the power of alliances.

So, whether you are a seasoned leader looking to strengthen your professional network or an individual seeking to enhance your personal relationships, *Unbreakable Alliances* will be your compass on this journey to success. Together, let us unlock the true potential of alliances and chart a course toward a future defined by collaboration, growth, and unbreakable bonds.

Ten Actions

1. Recognize the importance of alliances for personal and professional success.
2. Understand the impact of alliances on mental health and overall well-being.
3. Define an alliance as a relationship based on shared goals, needs, and support.
4. Learn guiding principles and expert techniques for creating unbreakable alliances.
5. Overcome trust challenges by understanding behaviors of trust and demonstrating trustworthiness.
6. Build trust by cultivating open and honest communication, transparency, and vulnerability.
7. Prioritize the needs and interests of others to build goodwill and trust.
8. Focus on building and maintaining a strong reputation for long-term success.
9. Embrace the responsibility of becoming a trusted ally and go-to person for others.
10. Practice active listening, tailor communication to others' priorities, embrace nonjudgmental curiosity, and empower others with choices to enhance communication and build unbreakable alliances.

2

TRUST

Building It, Keeping It

*A single act of kindness throws out roots in all directions,
and the roots spring up and make new trees.*
—Amelia Earhart

The Flight Connection That Changed Everything

It was a typical Monday afternoon, and I had settled into my seat on a crowded plane, surrounded by strangers, all lost in their own worlds. As the flight attendants prepared for takeoff, I couldn't help but notice the tension in the air, the invisible barriers that kept us isolated from one another.

Being the curious person that I am, I decided to break through those barriers. I turned to the man sitting next to me, a gentleman in a well-tailored suit, and with a friendly smile, I asked, "So, what brings you to be sitting here on this plane today?"

To my surprise, the man's eyes lit up, and he eagerly began sharing his story. He was a retired CEO traveling to a conference to give a presentation on executive leadership. As he passionately described his work and the challenges he faced, his voice exuded confidence and expertise.

During that short flight, something incredible happened. The invisible walls that had confined us as mere seatmates crumbled, replaced by an instant connection rooted in genuine curiosity and shared enthusiasm. By the time we landed, we had exchanged business cards, made plans to connect in the future, and laid the groundwork for what would become a valuable professional relationship.

Reflecting on that flight conversation, I couldn't help but realize the power of building rapport and trust in unexpected situations. It was a vivid reminder that the first impression we make, the fleeting moments we have to connect with others, hold the key to unlocking untapped potential and forging unbreakable alliances.

In the world of business leadership, every encounter, whether it's on a crowded plane or in a high-stakes meeting, presents an opportunity to build rapport and trust. This skill transcends titles and positions, enabling leaders to inspire, influence, and create lasting impact.

Beyond mere technique or strategy, however, building genuine connections requires a mindset shift—a commitment to authenticity, transparency, and empathy. It is about understanding that true leadership is not about manipulating others or controlling their actions but instead about creating an environment where trust can flourish and alliances can thrive.

Throughout this chapter, we will explore the importance of rapport and trust in business leadership. We will review effective techniques for establishing genuine connections, uncovering the power of nonverbal communication, active listening, and authenticity. Together, we will unlock the secrets to creating unbreakable alliances, grounded in trust and mutual respect.

Let us embark on this journey, drawing inspiration from my serendipitous flight connection, as we navigate the intricacies of building rapport and trust. May this chapter serve as a guiding light, illuminating the path to becoming a master of alliances and a true leader in the world of business.

The Power of Rapport and Trust in Business Leadership

Business leadership contains one fundamental truth that cannot be ignored: building rapport and trust is the cornerstone of creating unbreakable allies. It is the very essence of successful and effective leadership. But why is it so crucial? Why does the first impression matter so much? These are the questions we must explore if we want to master the art of creating unbreakable alliances.

When we engage with another human being, whether in a personal or professional setting, our brains are wired to assess for safety and trust. It is a survival trait, deeply ingrained within us. In the first thirty seconds (or even within milliseconds) of any interaction, we are subconsciously evaluating the other person's trustworthiness.

This assessment determines our level of comfort and willingness to engage further.

Now, let's consider the context of business leadership. As a leader, you have an agenda, a vision, and goals to accomplish. To achieve those goals, you must assess whether you can trust the people around you and build strong alliances with them. And that is where the power of rapport comes into play.

Rapport is the foundation upon which all successful relationships are built. Years ago, during my time at the FBI training academy, I developed a course and wrote a book titled *It's Not All About "Me": The Top 10 Techniques for Quick Rapport with Anyone.* In that course, I emphasized the importance of establishing genuine connections with others. It is a simple concept, yet one often overlooked.[1]

To truly connect with someone on a genuine and sincere level, we must abandon the notion of using interpersonal tricks or manipulative tactics. These techniques may provide short-term gains but are detrimental to extended trust and alliance building. When we employ strategies to control or deceive others, trust is shattered the moment our intentions are revealed. And once trust is broken, it is incredibly challenging to regain.

Instead, we must focus on building authentic connections, which requires transparency, honesty, and a genuine interest in the other person. This process is about understanding their needs, values, and aspirations. It is about listening actively and empathetically. It is about finding common ground and shared experiences. It is about creating an environment where trust can flourish.

So, how do we establish this genuine connection? The answer is simpler than we may think. It begins with a mindset shift. We must approach every interaction with the intention to understand and connect, rather than to manipulate and control. We must prioritize the well-being and trust of others above our own agenda.

Elsewhere, we will delve deeper into specific techniques and strategies for building rapport and trust in various business scenarios. We will explore the power of nonverbal communication, active listening, empathy, and authenticity. In addition, I will give you a toolkit of skills that will enable you to create unbreakable alliances, based on mutual trust and respect.

But remember, these techniques are not meant to be used as tricks or shortcuts. They are meant to be employed with integrity and genuine care for others. When we approach leadership with authenticity and a commitment to building rapport and trust, we unlock the true potential of our teams and ourselves.

Let's uncover together the guiding principles for success and expert techniques for creating unbreakable allies. I hope this will serve as your road map, guiding you toward becoming a master of rapport and trust in the world of business leadership.

Effective Techniques for Establishing Genuine Connection with Others

I've found that establishing deep and real connections with people is not as complicated as it may seem. The key is to be present in the moment and approach the conversation with genuine curiosity. Before the interaction, do as much homework and research as you can about the person, company, or organization you'll be working with. Once you're actually engaging with them, give them your undivided attention and be genuinely interested in what they have to say.

In *It's Not All About "Me,"* I discuss techniques that can enhance the encounter and make the other person feel safe and empowered. One is to establish time constraints. By setting a specific duration for the conversation or task, you let the other person know when it will end. This helps them feel safe by empowering them with knowledge and situational awareness. And if you can finish the task or conversation a bit earlier than expected, you've shown that you're clear, concise, and prompt, which builds your credibility and reliability.[2]

Thoughtfulness is another powerful technique for building rapport. It's amazing how something as simple as a handwritten thank-you note or showing knowledge of someone's interests can make a significant impact. By going the extra mile to show that you're paying attention and care about what matters to them, you strengthen the connection.

Curiosity is a valuable tool for building rapport as well. By being genuinely curious about the other person, you can establish commonalities and create a sense of affiliation. Even if you come from different backgrounds, you can always find shared experiences. During my time at the FBI, I interacted with people of various nationalities. Despite our cultural differences, we could always find common ground in our favorite foods or family traditions. Identifying and sharing these commonalities can spark a positive connection.

However, it's important to avoid making assumptions or sweeping generalizations. Each person is unique, and their life experiences shape them differently. Basing assumptions on generalizations can lead to misunderstandings and hinder the connection. Instead, approach conversations with an open mind and seek to understand the individual's thoughts and opinions.

By practicing these techniques, you can establish genuine connections with others and create unbreakable alliances. Remember, it's about being present, curious, and thoughtful while avoiding assumptions. These simple yet powerful strategies can make all the difference in building strong relationships.

The Code of Trust: Building Successful Alliances

Trust is the bedrock of any successful relationship, be it in the world of counterintelligence or in the world of business. Understanding and implementing the code of trust can help us navigate these complex dynamics and create unbreakable allies.

Let me share an anecdote from my time as the chief of the Behavioral Analysis Program. I was asked to write an article on counterintelligence for a law enforcement bulletin, and I wanted to find a way to explain what my team did without compromising national security. So, I decided to write about our role in the Behavioral Analysis Program, which involved strategizing operations for case agents.

As I sat down to compose this article, I realized that at the core of everything we did was human engagement. Regardless of the mission or objective, every interaction required a connection with another person. Our job was to strategize successful and healthy human engagement, essentially creating allies.

And what I discovered through contemplation was that all we were ever doing was strategizing trust. Trust is the foundation on which we inspire others to share information, cooperate with us, and take action. With this realization, I developed a five-step code of trust.

Step 1 is *understanding your goal*, the overarching objective you are trying to achieve. This includes identifying the common destination, the what and how, and most importantly, the who. Who needs to be part of your team in order to accomplish the goal?

Step 2 involves *discovering the priorities, needs, aspirations, wants, and dreams of the people you are engaging with*. Understanding their motivations and what makes them feel safe is crucial in building trust.

Step 3 is all about *exercising empathy and understanding people's context*. How do they see life through their own unique perspective? By practicing nonjudgmental curiosity, being open, and seeking to understand, we can discover what they want to share, rather than focusing solely on what we want to know.

Step 4 is about *communicating effectively*. We need to use the four keys of communication in all our interactions. Seek their thoughts and opinions, talk in terms of their priorities and challenges, validate them without judgment, and empower them with choices.

Last, step 5 is about *bringing it all together for meaningful engagement*. We do our homework, understand their life arc, and strategize one opening question that initiates a deep understanding of their journey and motivations. This question could be as simple as asking them about the spark or inspiration that made them who they are today.

Step 1: Understanding Your Goal

Let's say you are a project manager tasked with leading a cross-functional team to develop a new product for your company. Your goal is to successfully launch the product within a specified timeframe and budget while ensuring customer satisfaction and profitability.

To understand your goal, you need to identify the common destination for your team. This involves clearly defining the objectives and outcomes you want to achieve. In this case, it could be creating a high-quality product that meets market demand, generates revenue, and establishes your company as an industry leader.

Next, you need to determine the what and the how. What are the specific tasks, milestones, and deliverables required to reach your goal? How will you allocate resources, manage timelines, and overcome potential challenges? This includes developing a project plan, assigning responsibilities, and setting realistic expectations for your team.

But perhaps the most important aspect of step 1 is identifying the who. Who are the key stakeholders and team members that need to be involved to accomplish your goal? This could include people from departments as varied as design, engineering, marketing, and sales. Understanding the importance of each person's role and expertise can help you assemble a diverse and capable team ready to contribute to the success of the project.

By understanding your goal, determining the what and how, and identifying the who, you can lay a solid foundation for building trust and establishing a successful alliance among your team members. This clarity of purpose and alignment of objectives will guide your decision making and create a shared sense of purpose among the team, ultimately leading to a more efficient and effective project execution.

Step 2: Discovering Priorities, Needs, and Aspirations

Let's continue with the example of being a project manager developing a new product. To build trust and successful alliances with your team members, it's crucial to understand their priorities, needs, and aspirations.

Sarah, one of your team members, is a talented designer who is passionate about creating innovative and visually appealing products. By having a conversation with Sarah and actively listening to her, you discover that her priority is to ensure that the product design aligns with the brand's aesthetics and values. She also expresses her need for creative freedom and the opportunity to experiment with new design concepts.

Another team member, John, is an experienced engineer who values efficiency and technical excellence. Through discussions with John, you learn that his priority is to develop a product that is reliable, scalable, and meets all the technical requirements. He emphasizes the need for clear specifications and a well-defined development process to ensure smooth execution.

By understanding Sarah and John's priorities, you can align their needs with the overall project goal. You can provide Sarah with the creative freedom she desires while setting clear design guidelines that align with the brand's vision. For John, you can establish a structured development process that ensures technical excellence while allowing him to contribute his expertise and insights.

In addition to understanding their priorities, you also should discover their aspirations and long-term goals. Sarah may aspire to be recognized as a leading designer in the industry, while John may have a goal of becoming a technical expert in his field. By acknowledging and supporting their aspirations, you can create an environment that fosters growth and development for both team members.

Taking time to discover the priorities, needs, and aspirations of your team members will help you build trust and demonstrate that you value their contributions. This understanding allows you to tailor your leadership approach, provide necessary support, and create an environment where each team member feels motivated and empowered to contribute their best work.

Step 3: Understanding Their Context

Continuing with the project manager example, let's focus on understanding the context of your team members to build trust and successful alliances.

One team member, April, is a junior designer who recently joined the company. To understand her context, you engage in a conversation with her to gain insights into her background and experiences. Through this dialogue, you discover that April recently graduated from design school and is eager to apply her skills and learn from more experienced team members. She shares that she values guidance and mentorship, as she wants to grow professionally and gain confidence in her abilities.

Another team member, Mike, is a senior engineer who has been with the company for several years. To understand his context, you engage in active listening and ask open-ended questions. Mike reveals that he has a family and is balancing work commitments with his personal responsibilities. He values work–life balance and appreciates flexibility in his schedule to accommodate his family's needs.

By understanding April's context, you can provide her with the support and guidance she needs as a junior designer. You can assign her a mentor who can provide valuable insights and help her develop her skills. You also can create opportunities for her to collaborate with more experienced team members and learn from their expertise.

With Mike, understanding his context allows you to be flexible and supportive of his work–life balance. You can explore options such as flexible working hours or remote work arrangements to accommodate his family responsibilities. By demonstrating empathy and understanding, you create an environment where Mike feels valued and motivated to contribute his best work.

Understanding the context of your team members goes beyond their professional roles. It involves recognizing their individual circumstances, aspirations, and challenges. By practicing nonjudgmental curiosity and being present in conversations, you can gain a deeper understanding of their perspectives and tailor your leadership approach accordingly.

Acknowledging and understanding the context of your team members helps you build trust and show that you genuinely care about their well-being and success. This leads to stronger alliances, increased engagement, and a collaborative work environment where everyone feels valued and supported.

Step 4: Effective Communication

In our project manager example, step 4 involves using the four keys of communication to build trust and successful alliances among your team.

One team member, Catherine, is a marketing specialist responsible for promoting the new product. As the project manager, you understand the importance of effective communication to align Catherine's efforts with the project goals and ensure a cohesive marketing strategy.

Using the four keys of communication, you engage with Catherine in the following ways:

1. *Seeking her thoughts and opinions*: Instead of dictating marketing strategies, you encourage Catherine to share her insights and ideas. You ask for her thoughts on target audiences, messaging, and promotional channels. By valuing her expertise and involving her in the decision-making process, you empower Catherine to contribute her unique perspective.

2. *Talking in terms of her priorities, challenges, and pain points*: You understand that Catherine's main priority is to drive customer engagement and generate leads for the new product. In communicating with her, you emphasize how marketing efforts can directly address these goals. You discuss potential challenges, such as budget constraints or competition, and brainstorm together on strategies to overcome them.

3. *Practicing nonjudgmental curiosity*: As Catherine presents her ideas and proposals, you provide constructive feedback and validation. You acknowledge the value of her contributions and express appreciation for her efforts. By creating a nonjudgmental environment, you cultivate open communication and trust.

4. *Empowering her with choices*: When discussing marketing tactics and campaigns, you involve Catherine in decision-making processes. You present her with different options and encourage her to make choices based on her expertise and knowledge. By giving her autonomy and responsibility, you empower Catherine to take ownership of her work.

Through effective communication using the four keys, you create a collaborative and trust-based relationship with Catherine. She feels heard, valued, and motivated to contribute her best to the marketing efforts for the new product.

By applying the four keys of communication with each team member, you ensure that interactions are focused on their perspectives, needs, and objectives. This leads to clearer understanding, better goal alignment, and a shared commitment to the project's success. Effective communication strengthens trust and fosters successful alliances within the team.

Step 5: Meaningful Engagement

In our project manager example, step 5 involves crafting a meaningful engagement with your team members by understanding their life arc and initiating a deep conversation. Let's focus on one team member, Peter, who is a software developer responsible for coding the new product.

As the project manager, you recognize the importance of establishing a strong connection with Peter to build trust and grow a successful alliance. To initiate a meaningful engagement, you strategically plan one opening question that taps into their life arc and motivations.

You sit down with Peter and start the conversation by asking, "Throughout your career as a software developer, what inspired you to pursue this path and your passion for coding?"

This question allows Peter to reflect on their journey and motivations, giving you valuable insights into their background and aspirations. As Peter shares their story, you actively listen, expressing genuine curiosity and interest.

Peter reveals that from a young age, they have always been fascinated by technology and have enjoyed solving complex problems. They express a deep passion for coding and the satisfaction it brings when they can turn ideas into functional software. They also mention their desire to continuously learn and stay up to date with the latest advancements in the field.

By understanding Peter's life arc, you gain a deeper understanding of their motivations and what drives their commitment to their work. This knowledge allows you to tailor your leadership approach to support their growth and provide meaningful opportunities for them to expand their skills.

Throughout the project, you speak periodically with Peter, checking on their progress, providing feedback, and discussing challenges and opportunities. By being present, attentive, and genuinely interested, you demonstrate that you value their contributions and are invested in their success.

This meaningful engagement with Peter not only builds trust but also strengthens the alliance between you as the project manager and them as a key team member. They feel understood, supported, and motivated to deliver their best work for the success of the project.

By applying step 5 and crafting a meaningful engagement with each team member, you establish a deep connection based on understanding and shared goals. This cultivates a collaborative and productive work environment where everyone feels valued and empowered to contribute their unique skills and talents.

Further, by following the code of trust and implementing these five steps, we can build strong alliances and establish trust with others. Remember, trust is not just a concept reserved for the world of counterintelligence. It is applicable in every aspect of life, including business and leadership.

As you launch your journey to create unbreakable allies, keep the code of trust in mind. Understand your goals, discover the priorities of others, empathize with their context, communicate effectively, and engage meaningfully. This code will guide you toward success in building trust and forging powerful alliances.

Overcoming Skepticism: Building Trust One Step at a Time

Skepticism can be a formidable obstacle when it comes to building trust in any alliance or partnership. It's natural for people to approach new relationships with caution, especially in the business world where the stakes can be high. However, if we want to create unbreakable allies, we must learn how to overcome skepticism and build trust despite initial doubt.

To address skepticism effectively, simplicity is key. It's important to understand that you cannot force someone to abandon their skepticism or reluctance. However, you can influence their perception of you and your intentions through consistent messaging and behavior. By being mindful of the way you communicate and interact with others, you can gradually chip away at their skepticism.

One crucial factor to consider is the concept of building a reservoir of goodwill. Every alliance you form is an opportunity to fill this reservoir. You can do this by becoming a valuable resource for others, taking the time to understand their challenges, priorities, and pain points, and offering assistance in solving them. This approach both demonstrates your genuine interest in their success and helps establish a foundation of trust.

But what about skepticism? Think of skepticism as a reservoir with leaks or holes. These leaks prevent the reservoir from being filled, and you cannot begin to withdraw from it until the leaks are plugged. The key to plugging those holes lies in consistency, patience, and careful observation of the other person's nonverbal cues and behaviors.

When you notice that their skepticism is starting to wane, that's when you can cautiously start making small withdrawals from the reservoir of trust. Ask for a favor or make a small request. However, you must proceed with caution and only make these asks when you can clearly see a positive shift in their nonverbal behavior.

Recognizing these behavioral shifts requires keen observation and an understanding of human communication. Look for signs of increased openness, such as relaxed body language, more frequent eye contact, or a genuine smile. These all indicate that the other person's skepticism is starting to diminish, and that the time may be right to slightly tap the reservoir of trust.

Remember, building trust takes time and effort. It requires consistent messaging, genuine care for others' needs, and patience. By approaching skepticism with a strategic and observant mindset, you can gradually overcome it and build unbreakable alliances based on trust and mutual benefit.

The Power of Active Listening

In our fast-paced world, it's easy to get caught up in our own thoughts, agendas, and to-do lists. We often overlook one of the most fundamental skills for success: active listening. It may sound simple, but truly listening to others is a skill that can make or break your ability to build strong alliances and achieve your goals.

So, what exactly is active listening? It's not just about hearing someone's words or nodding along to their conversation. Active listening is about focusing your energy and attention on someone else, truly understanding their perspective, and making them feel valued and heard. It's about being present in the moment and letting go of your own biases and preconceived notions.

Many techniques and strategies have been taught for active listening, such as repeating the last word the person said, paraphrasing their statements, or mirroring their nonverbal behavior. While these techniques can be helpful, they can also distract us from truly listening and paying attention to what the other person is saying and doing.

Research has shown that human beings cannot effectively multitask. When we try to focus on what we should be doing as active listeners, we actually miss out on important details and cues from the other person. Our minds are too preoccupied with our own agenda, preventing us from fully engaging in the conversation.[3]

To truly practice active listening, we need to do our homework beforehand. We should invest time and effort in understanding the individual, the situation, and all the nuances that will contribute to a meaningful conversation. This preparation sets the stage for a great engagement, allowing us to build rapport and trust.

However, when we are in the moment, we must let go of our agenda and the need to control the conversation. We also need to release our confirmation bias—the tendency to look for things that align with our beliefs or expectations. Instead, we should be fully present, open minded, and receptive to what the other person is saying.

When we let go of our agenda, we create space for true understanding and connection. We become attuned to the nuances in the other person's words and actions, picking up on important details we otherwise might have missed. This is where the magic of active listening happens—when we truly hear and see things that are important to the other person.

In her book *Insight*, Tasha Eurich emphasizes the importance of being present and fully attentive in conversations. Simon Sinek echoes this sentiment in his books on leadership by highlighting the power of listening and understanding as key traits of effective leaders. As leaders, it is our responsibility to create an environment where others feel heard and valued.[4]

Imagine you're a sales manager attending a conference where you have the opportunity to meet potential clients and build new alliances. As you mingle with the attendees, you come across a person named Parker who runs a successful marketing agency. You've done your homework and know that Parker's agency specializes in social media marketing, an area your company is looking to explore.

Instead of jumping right into a sales pitch or talking about your company's needs, you decide to practice active listening. You ask Parker open-ended questions about her agency, her experiences in the industry, and her thoughts on the latest trends in social media marketing. You genuinely show interest in her responses, nodding along and maintaining eye contact.

As the conversation progresses, you notice Parker's enthusiasm and passion for her work. She shares a recent campaign she successfully ran for a client, and you pick up on her pride in achieving tangible results. You make mental notes of these details, recognizing the importance of understanding her perspective and appreciating her expertise.

By actively listening, you create an environment where Parker feels valued and heard. She begins to open up about the challenges she faces in the industry and her aspirations for the future. You empathize with her struggles, acknowledging the ever-changing social media landscape and the need for innovative strategies.

Toward the end of the conversation, Parker asks about your company's goals and how you envision working with marketing agencies like hers. You seize the opportunity to align your objectives with hers, highlighting the potential for collaboration and emphasizing the value your company places on expertise and creativity.

Thanks to your active listening skills, Parker feels a genuine connection with and trust toward you. She recognizes that you've taken the time to understand her and her agency's needs, and she sees the potential for a fruitful partnership. You exchange contact information, promising to follow up with more details and potential opportunities.

In this example, active listening played a crucial role in building rapport, trust, and ultimately creating an unbreakable alliance. By genuinely showing interest, letting go of your own agenda, and fully engaging in the conversation, you were able to establish a connection with Parker and position your company as a valuable collaborator.

To become a successful leader and create unbreakable alliances, remember the power of active listening. Practice letting go of your own agenda and truly immersing yourself in the moment. Invest the time to understand others and be fully present when engaging in conversations. By doing so, you will build strong relationships, gain valuable insights, and pave the way for success in your business endeavors.

Harnessing the Power of Nonverbal Cues for Building Trust

In the realm of professional relationships, our ability to foster trust and create unbreakable allies relies heavily on our mastery of nonverbal communication and body language. Nonverbal cues can be powerful tools for establishing rapport and conveying our intentions, but they must be used effectively to induce comfort rather than stress.

Distinguishing between reactions of stress and comfort is essential to understanding the impact of nonverbal cues. Renowned nonverbal-communication expert Mark Bowden aptly describes stress as being bundled up in a freezing, wintry environment, shivering and clenching our bodies tightly to conserve warmth. This physical response mirrors the nonverbal behaviors associated with stress—clothes can feel tight and cramped, and the body becomes restricted in its movement. In contrast, comfort is akin to entering a warm, inviting log cabin with a roaring fire and a cup of hot chocolate waiting for us. As we shed our more constricting winter attire, we open our bodies up to the warmth and relaxation of the environment as we shed those heavy clothes. Nonverbal displays of comfort mirror this state of ease—our bodies are relaxed, open, and expansive.[5]

To effectively use nonverbal cues to build trust, we must assess our own behaviors and ensure that we are inducing comfort instead of stress. Before we can access the reservoir of goodwill, we must first fill it with an abundance of comforting nonverbal displays. Stress indicators can deplete this reservoir and hinder our ability to build trust.

Congruence is another vital aspect of nonverbal communication that we must emphasize. Incongruence, or a disconnect between what is being said and the nonverbal cues being emitted, can make people feel uneasy or uncomfortable. Have you ever experienced a business interaction where something just didn't feel right or gave you a creepy feeling? Chances are there was incongruence between the person's words and their nonverbal behavior.

To be congruent, we must genuinely believe that we are there to solve a problem, address a challenge, or alleviate a pain point for the other person. Our nonverbal cues should naturally reflect this mindset, aligning with our words and feelings. When we are congruent, our nonverbal cues become a powerful force in building trust and rapport.

Recognizing incongruence in others is equally important. We must be attuned to the nonverbal cues of those we interact with, as incongruence can erode trust and hinder the establishment of strong alliances. By honing our ability to read and understand nonverbal cues, we can navigate professional relationships with greater insight and effectiveness.

Nonverbal communication and body language are crucial components of building trust and creating unbreakable allies. By inducing comfort through our nonverbal cues and maintaining congruence between our words and actions, we can develop trust and forge strong professional relationships. Understanding and using the power of nonverbal communication is a key principle for success in the realm of business leadership.

Building Credibility and Reliability

Two more traits at the core of trust are credibility and reliability. Credibility is all about consistency. It is about repeatedly demonstrating that you are someone who can be relied upon. It is about showing up consistently, delivering on your promises, and exceeding expectations. When leaders consistently overperform and consistently deliver results, they build credibility. It is not about a one-time success or a single act of excellence. It is about a pattern of behavior that inspires confidence in others.

Reliability, on the other hand, is about being able to produce in a consistent, useful way. It is about being someone who can be counted on to get the job done, no matter the circumstances. Reliability is about being dependable in your actions and behaviors. When leaders consistently demonstrate their ability to deliver on their commitments and produce tangible results, they build reliability. It is not just about saying the right things, but also about following through with action.

Establishing credibility and reliability as a leader arises from adopting specific actions and behaviors. Here are a few key strategies:

1. *Consistency in Actions*: Be consistent in your actions and behaviors. This means showing up regularly, following through on your commitments, and being reliable in all that you do. Consistency builds trust and establishes you as a credible and reliable leader.

2. *Transparency and Open Communication*: Sharing information widely and clearly builds trust and shows that you have nothing to hide. When leaders are open and honest in their communication, they establish credibility and reliability.

3. *Accountability*: Take responsibility for your actions. Leaders build credibility and reliability by owning their mistakes and learning from them. Being accountable shows that you can be trusted to do the right thing, even when things go wrong.

4. *Deliver Results*: Consistently deliver results and exceed expectations. When leaders consistently produce tangible results, it establishes credibility and reliability. It shows that you are someone who can be counted on to get the job done.

5. *Build Relationships*: Invest time and effort into building strong relationships with others. Leaders build credibility and reliability by taking the time to understand the needs and concerns of their team members and stakeholders. It shows that you care about others and are committed to their success.

Building credibility and reliability takes time and effort. It requires consistent actions and behaviors that demonstrate trustworthiness. By following these strategies, leaders can lay the foundation for strong and unbreakable alliances.

Leveraging Shared Experiences and Interests for Building Unbreakable Alliances

One powerful tool that leaders can harness to forge unbreakable connections is shared experiences and interests. By leveraging these commonalities, leaders can create a sense of rapport, understanding, and trust among their team members and potential allies. In this section, we will explore the various ways leaders can utilize shared experiences and interests to strengthen their alliances.

Building Traditions

Traditions have a remarkable ability to bring people together. Leaders can establish organizational traditions such as company picnics, outings, or conferences. These recurring events provide team members with opportunities to bond over shared experiences. By participating in these traditions together, team members can develop a sense of camaraderie and unity, forming the foundation of unbreakable alliances.

Personal Histories and Traditions

On an individual level, leaders can delve into the personal histories and traditions of their team members or potential allies. By showing genuine interest and curiosity, leaders can create a safe space for sharing stories, experiences, and cultural backgrounds. This not only fosters a deeper understanding but also allows for the discovery of shared experiences or traditions that can strengthen the alliance.

In my book *Sizing People Up*, I shared the story of Anan, a confidential human source I recruited for the FBI after 9/11. During our initial conversations, I asked Anan about his favorite family traditions growing up. He shared his love for Kashmiri tea and simple flatbread with lentils cooked on a hot stone. Intrigued by his stories, I made sure to have Kashmiri tea prepared for our next meeting. From there, we began sharing our favorite meals and foods, creating a unique bonding experience that transcended our different backgrounds. Through this exchange of traditions, we formed a strong alliance built on mutual respect and understanding.[6]

Creating Inclusive Environments

Leaders can encourage a sense of belonging and inclusivity by acknowledging and celebrating the diverse backgrounds and traditions of their team members. By taking time to learn about different cultures, customs, and experiences, leaders demonstrate their commitment to creating an environment where everyone feels valued and respected. They can strengthen alliances while encouraging team members to bring their whole selves to work, leading to increased engagement and collaboration.

Organizing Activities Based on Shared Interests

Another effective way to leverage shared experiences and interests is by organizing team-building activities that revolve around common hobbies or passions. Whether it's a hiking trip, a cooking class, or a book club, these activities provide team members with opportunities to connect on a deeper level outside of the office. Engaging in shared interests fosters a sense of camaraderie and can create lasting memories that strengthen alliances.

Shared experiences and interests serve as powerful tools for building unbreakable alliances in the business world. By leveraging traditions, exploring personal histories, creating inclusive environments, and organizing activities based on shared interests, leaders can forge deep connections and cultivate a culture of collaboration and trust. When leaders prioritize building alliances through shared experiences, they set their teams and organizations up for long-term success.

Building Rapport and Trust: Overcoming the Obstacles

Leaders face numerous challenges when it comes to building rapport and trust with others. One of the most significant obstacles they encounter is when they have a self-serving agenda, and subconsciously or consciously place their own goals ahead of those with whom they wish to develop rapport. Life is filled with many dichotomies, opposing forces that shape our interactions and relationships. To successfully forge alliances and establish trust, leaders must navigate this delicate balance of our needs and the needs of others with finesse.

When entering into a new relationship, we often lack the credibility necessary to balance the dichotomy. Building up a reservoir of trust is essential, and we can only achieve this by initially focusing more on the other person and their needs than on our own. Letting go of personal agendas and refraining from making immediate asks are crucial in this early stage.

In addition, observing nonverbal cues and engaging in meaningful conversations are valuable tools in gauging the readiness of the other person to achieve a deeper level of trust and rapport. When they begin to ask you about your thoughts, opinions, and ideas, and seek your insights on their own challenges, priorities, and pain points, they are clearly indicating that the reservoir of trust is beginning to fill.

At this stage, they might even offer resources to help you overcome your own challenges. This is a significant milestone, as it demonstrates that you have successfully inspired them to become a resource for you, reinforcing the bond of trust and rapport.

Overcoming the obstacle of pursuing a self-serving agenda requires patience, selflessness, and the ability to establish a genuine connection. It is not about manipulating or coercing others into doing what we want, but rather about understanding their needs, empathizing with their challenges, and offering support without any immediate expectation in return.

Leaders who can embrace this approach and prioritize the building of trust and rapport will find themselves creating unbreakable alliances that can weather any storm. By focusing on others before themselves, leaders can establish a solid foundation of trust, enabling them to succeed in their own endeavors while guiding and inspiring their allies to reach their full potential.

Remember, building rapport and trust is a journey that requires continuous effort and commitment. But by adopting these guiding principles and expert techniques, you can navigate the challenges and obstacles that come your way, and create unbreakable alliances that will propel you toward success.

The Power of Focusing on Others

Have you ever found yourself so focused on your own goals and aspirations that you neglected those around you? I know I have. In fact, I used to be that hard-charging, type-A individual who was constantly striving for success and recognition. I wanted to be the best, to achieve great things, and to have everyone see how capable I was. But in my pursuit of personal greatness, I failed to realize the true power of focusing on others.

Looking back, if there's one piece of advice I could give my twenty-year-old self, it would be this: instead of focusing solely on my own dreams and goals, I should have been paying attention to the people around me. I should have been asking myself, "How can I make their lives easier? How can I help them succeed?"

You see, true leadership isn't about being in the spotlight or achieving personal accolades. It's about being a proactive resource for others' success without expecting anything in return. It's about making a positive impact on the lives of those around you.

When you shift your focus from yourself to others, amazing things happen. People notice. They appreciate your support and genuine interest in their well-being. They start to see you as someone they can rely on, someone who makes their day a little bit easier and a little bit better.

Imagine being the person that everyone can't wait to see walk through the door or have reach out to them. Imagine being the person who brings a sense of relief and positivity to their lives. That is the power of becoming a powerful ally.

My advice to aspiring business leaders who want to excel in trust and create unbreakable allies is simple: focus on those around you.

Take the time to understand their dreams, aspirations, and goals. Discover what their jobs entail and how you can make their lives smoother and more successful. Be the person who goes above and beyond to help others without expecting anything in return.

Remember, true leadership is not about how high you can climb, but about how many people you can uplift along the way. And when you become someone who genuinely cares about others' success, you will find yourself surrounded by unbreakable allies who are willing to support you in return.

Ten Actions

1. Prioritize building rapport and trust in your interactions with others, both personally and professionally.
2. Shift your mindset to prioritize understanding and connecting with others rather than controlling or manipulating them.
3. Commit to acting with integrity and avoid employing manipulative strategies in your leadership approach.
4. Practice active listening by giving others your full attention, asking open-ended questions, and seeking to understand their perspective.
5. Reflect on your leadership style and strive to lead with authenticity, transparency, and a commitment to building rapport and trust.
6. Practice active listening and being fully present in conversations. Put away distractions and focus on the person

you're speaking with. Ask open-ended questions to show genuine curiosity and encourage them to share more.

7. Research and gather information about any person, company, or organization you will be meeting with. Use online resources, social media, and professional networks to gain insights that will help you understand their background, goals, and challenges.

8. Implement time constraints for your conversations and meetings. Before beginning a discussion, communicate how long you expect it to take. This sets clear expectations and empowers the other person by telling them when the conversation will end.

9. Practice thoughtfulness in your interactions by going above and beyond. Send handwritten thank-you notes or emails expressing gratitude for someone's time or help. Take note of important events in their lives, such as birthdays or work anniversaries, and acknowledge them with a thoughtful message or small gesture.

10. Cultivate curiosity and actively look for commonalities in your conversations. Ask open-ended questions that allow the other person to share their experiences and interests. When you find shared experiences or interests, use them as conversation starters and ways to connect on a deeper level. However, be mindful of not basing assumptions solely on these commonalities, and stay open to discovering each individual's unique perspective.

3

COMMUNICATE

The Golden Key to Success

Tell me and I forget, teach me and I may remember, involve me and I learn.
—Benjamin Franklin

The Power of Understanding the Listener

As I stepped into the FBI Counterintelligence Training Center, I was filled with a sense of purpose. I was there to teach, to share my knowledge and experiences, and to mold the next generation of FBI agents and leaders. Little did I know that a single moment would forever change the way I approached communication.

In one of my early classes, I found myself pouring my heart and soul into delivering the valuable information I had accumulated over the years. But as I scanned the room, something didn't feel right. Not all of my students were fully engaged. Some seemed distant, their minds elsewhere. It left me perplexed, wondering what I had missed.

Determined to uncover the truth, I sought the guidance of a trusted mentor and friend. He graciously agreed to observe one of my classes, and afterward, he posed a question that sent ripples through my mind: "Did you happen to notice the response when you were speaking and sharing that valuable information?"

His words made me pause and reflect on the varying reactions I had witnessed. It was then that I realized the importance of delivering information in a way that resonates with the listener. It wasn't enough to have valuable knowledge; I also needed to adapt my approach to meet the needs and preferences of my audience.

This revelation became the foundation of my philosophy for effective communication while creating unbreakable alliances. It shifted my focus from merely sharing what I wanted to impart, to understanding what others wanted to receive. Seeking their thoughts, talking in their language, validating their perspectives, and empowering them with choices became the guiding principles of my teachings. I highlighted these keys to communication earlier, and they will continue to resonate throughout our journey.

To truly grasp the essence of this revelation, I embarked on a transformative journey. I immersed myself in the same information my listeners consumed, seeking to understand their perspectives, opinions, and communication preferences. This empathy-driven approach allowed me to tailor my delivery, making the information resonate on a deeper level.

In this chapter, we will delve into the principles behind this revelation, with the goal of equipping you with the tools and techniques to revolutionize your communication skills. By embracing empathy and focusing on others' needs, you will unlock the secrets to forging connections that transcend boundaries and create unbreakable alliances.

It's time for you to begin your own journey of transformation. Together, we will navigate the path to success, leaving behind ordinary interactions and embracing extraordinary opportunities. Are you ready to dive in and discover the true power of communication?

The Power of Empathy in Building Alliances

Empathy is the key that unlocks the door to understanding and connecting with others more deeply. It allows us to see the world through someone else's lens, to understand their context and experiences, and to communicate with them in a way that resonates with them.

Empathy goes beyond mere compassion or kindness. It is about truly stepping into someone else's shoes and viewing the world from their perspective. It requires us to consider their social status and economic background, and the demographic factors that shape their lives. By doing so, we gain valuable insights into their motivations, needs, and desires.

One of my favorite authors, Ryan Holiday, who writes extensively on Stoicism, highlights the importance of empathy in problem solving. With its emphasis on rationality and practicality, Stoicism provides a perfect framework for practicing empathy. By understanding the world through someone else's lens, we can better grasp the challenges they face and find effective solutions to their problems.[1]

In the realm of business leadership, empathy becomes a powerful tool for communication. When you are trying to lead a group or organization, it is not enough to communicate your ideas in terms of why *you* think they are important. Instead, you must be able to communicate in terms of why your *audience* would find them important. This is where empathy comes into play.

By empathizing with your team members, colleagues, or clients, you can tailor your communication to their specific needs and perspectives. You can articulate your objectives in a way that resonates with them, highlighting the benefits and values that align with their own interests. This approach not only fosters better understanding but also creates a sense of shared purpose and commitment.

For example, let's say you are leading a team and need to communicate a new strategic direction. Instead of simply presenting your ideas and expecting others to follow, you can take a step back and empathize with your team members. Understand their concerns, motivations, and aspirations. By doing so, you can frame your message in a way that addresses their needs and shows how the new direction aligns with their individual and collective goals.

By incorporating empathy into your leadership approach, you can create a culture of trust, collaboration, and mutual respect within your organization. You can build genuine connections with your team members and stakeholders, creating a strong foundation for lasting alliances. Empathy enables you to navigate the complexities of diverse perspectives, bridge communication gaps, and find common ground even in the face of disagreement.

Empathy is a vital skill for leaders seeking to create unbreakable alliances. By practicing empathy, leaders can build stronger relationships, nurture collaboration, and inspire others to join them on the path to success. However, effective communication goes beyond just empathy. In the next section, we will explore the different communication styles that leaders can employ to enhance their alliance-building efforts.

Tailoring Communication Styles for Effective Communication

Understanding and adapting to different communication styles is essential for effective leadership. People have varying preferences for how they give and receive information, and being able to recognize and adjust to these preferences is crucial for building strong alliances. One tool that can help in this endeavor is the DISC personality profile, which provides insights into different communication styles.

The DISC profile, developed by William Moulton Marston in the 1920s and 1930s, is a widely used assessment that measures individuals' communication preferences. It categorizes people into four main quadrants based on two dichotomies: dominance versus influence and conscientiousness versus steadiness.[2]

- In the top-left quadrant, we have the *dominant drivers*, who are task oriented and direct. These individuals are assertive, unafraid to take charge, and focused on getting things done.
- In the top-right quadrant, we have *influential influencers*, who are people oriented and direct. Influencers are social, outgoing, and love to generate ideas and engage in discussions.

- In the bottom-right quadrant, we have the *steady relators* who are people oriented and indirect. These individuals are supportive, value relationships, and prefer to work in a collaborative manner.
- Last, in the bottom-left quadrant, we have the *conscientious thinkers*, who are task oriented and indirect. Detail minded and organized, they prefer to follow rules.

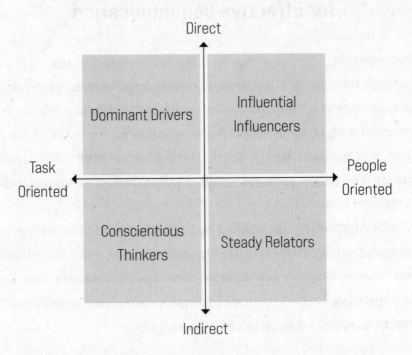

While each of us may have a dominant style, we all possess a blend of these communication preferences. When under stress or pressure, however, we tend to default to our dominant style. Recognizing and understanding these preferences in others can help us tailor our communication style to effectively engage with them.

You can identify individuals' communication styles through observation. Pay attention to how they structure conversations, how they organize their desks or homes, and even how they approach tasks like grocery shopping or vacation planning. These behaviors can provide valuable insights into how they prefer to communicate.

One strategy for better assessing the communication style of the person we are interacting with is to slow down and think before speaking. Listen more and talk less. Then, we can shift our approach by sorting individuals into dominance-oriented or influence-oriented categories.

For instance, provide clear instructions and concise information to dominance-oriented individuals. They appreciate directness and efficiency, so being direct will resonate with them. On the other hand, influence-oriented individuals value personal connections and stories. Taking the time to engage in conversations and discussing the people involved in a task will help create a stronger rapport.

Misinterpreting someone's communication style can lead to misunderstandings and frustration. Treating an influence-oriented person as if they are dominance oriented by giving them a quick checklist might come across as impersonal and disconnected. Similarly, approaching a dominance-oriented person as if they are influence oriented by engaging in lengthy discussions and personal anecdotes can be seen as a waste of time.

To employ effective communication, you need to assess how someone prefers to give and receive information. By delivering the same information in a way that is tailored to their preferences, we can deepen our understanding and build stronger alliances.

DISC in Action

Once upon a time in a bustling office, there was a team of four individuals who perfectly embodied the different DISC profiles. Let's meet them!

First, there was Dominic, the dominant driver. Dominic was known for his no-nonsense approach and his relentless drive to achieve results. One day, the team was tasked with organizing a company-wide event. Dominic took charge immediately, creating a detailed plan with strict deadlines and assigning tasks to each team member. He made it clear that efficiency and productivity were his top priorities.

Next, we have Isabella, the influential influencer. Isabella was the life of the office, always full of energy and ideas. When the team gathered to discuss the event, Isabella lit up the room with her creativity. She suggested fun icebreaker activities, entertaining performances, and even a theme that would make the event memorable. Isabella's enthusiasm was contagious, and everyone felt excited to be a part of her vision.

Then there was Ryan, the steady relator. Ryan was known for his calm and supportive nature. As the team worked on the event, Ryan took the time to listen to each team member's ideas and concerns. He made sure everyone felt heard and valued, which fostered a collaborative atmosphere. Ryan was the glue that held the team together, ensuring that relationships were nurtured along the way.

Last but not least, we have Claire, the conscientious thinker. Claire was the detail-oriented member of the team, known for her meticulous planning and adherence to rules. She created a checklist that covered every aspect of the event, from logistics to budgeting. Claire's ability to dot every "i" and cross every "t" ensured that the event would run smoothly without any hiccups.

As the event day approached, the team realized they needed to bring all their communication styles together to make it a success. Dominic's task-oriented approach ensured that everything was organized and on schedule. Isabella's influence-oriented ideas brought excitement and engagement to the event. Ryan's people-oriented nature created a warm and welcoming atmosphere. And Claire's attention to detail ensured that nothing was overlooked.

On the day of the event, the office buzzed with anticipation. Thanks to the combined efforts of Dominic, Isabella, Ryan, and Claire, the event was a roaring success. The attendees had a fantastic time, and the team received praise for their hard work and coordination.

The anecdote of this diverse team highlights the power of understanding and adapting to different communication styles. Each member's unique strengths and preferences contributed to the overall success of the event. By recognizing and appreciating the different DISC profiles, they were able to work harmoniously and achieve great things together.

The moral of the story: In the world of communication and teamwork, embracing diverse communication styles, as represented by the DISC profiles, and tailoring one's interactions and team assignments to them, can lead to incredible outcomes—and a lot of fun along the way! By recognizing and adjusting to others' communication styles, leaders can build unbreakable alliances and achieve success.

The Power of Nonverbal Cues in Communication

In the previous chapter, we discussed harnessing the power of nonverbal cues for building trust. These cues provide valuable insights into a person's true thoughts and feelings. By understanding and leveraging these cues, we can enhance our ability to create unbreakable alliances.

When assessing our communication effectiveness, it is essential to look for congruence between a person's spoken language and their body language. We want their words and nonverbal cues to align and reinforce each other. This congruence signifies authenticity and trustworthiness, both crucial elements in building successful alliances.

To assess someone's congruence, we need to closely observe their interactions. Pay attention to their body language throughout the conversation. Are they maintaining a consistent posture and demeanor? Do their gestures and facial expressions align with their spoken words? These are essential cues that can help us gauge their level of comfort and openness.

We also explored in the "Trust" chapter the analogy of coming in from the freezing cold and finding oneself in a warm, cozy room. Shedding the layers that kept us warm outside, we sit down with a cup of hot cocoa, allowing our bodies to absorb the warmth and creating a feeling of deep comfort. We should strive to create this kind of comfort in our communication.

Likewise, when assessing our own communication effectiveness while speaking with someone, we should aim to maintain our initial body language and improve upon it as the conversation progresses. We want our nonverbal cues to align with our spoken words and convey a sense of ease and authenticity. This alignment will build trust and rapport, laying the foundation for unbreakable alliances.

Moreover, interpreting others' nonverbal cues allows us to gain deeper insights into their thoughts and emotions. By observing their body language, we can discern whether they are truly engaged and receptive to our message. Are they leaning in attentively? Maintaining eye contact? Matching our tempo? These cues can indicate genuine interest and a willingness to collaborate.

Once we interpret these nonverbal cues, we can respond accordingly to strengthen the alliance. For example, if we notice signs of discomfort or disinterest, we can adjust our communication approach to re-engage the person. By adapting our body language and communication style, we can create a more comfortable and inclusive environment that encourages open dialogue and collaboration.

Nonverbal cues play a crucial role in effective communication. By assessing congruence between spoken language and body language, we can gauge our own communication effectiveness and strive for greater authenticity. Additionally, interpreting nonverbal cues from others allows us to understand their true thoughts and emotions, enabling us to respond and adapt our communication approach accordingly. By mastering the art of nonverbal communication, we can create unbreakable alliances based on trust, authenticity, and mutual understanding.

The Power of Emotional Intelligence in Business Communication

Emotional intelligence (EQ) is a crucial factor in effective communication, especially in the context of business leadership. EQ is the ability to recognize, understand, and manage our own emotions, as well as empathize with and respond effectively to the emotions of others. Renowned psychologist Daniel Goleman introduced the concept of EQ in a book by that title that highlights its five key elements: self-awareness, self-regulation, motivation, empathy, and social skills.[3]

1. *Self-awareness* involves recognizing and understanding
    our own emotions, strengths, weaknesses, and values.
    While self-awareness is essential, focusing excessively on
    it can lead to a lack of empathy and self-regulation. For
    instance, if we have been conditioned to rely solely on our
    own resilience and self-reliance, our self-awareness might
    become overpowering. To mitigate this, we can add empathy
    and self-regulation to our repertoire.

2. *Self-regulation* is about managing and controlling our
    emotions, impulses, and behaviors. By developing self-
    regulation, we can avoid letting our emotions dictate
    our actions, especially in high-pressure situations. Self-
    regulation counterbalances self-awareness, tempering any
    excessive self-focus.

3. *Motivation* drives us to achieve personal goals and channel
    our emotions toward productivity and success. It is the
    force that propels us forward, especially during challenging
    times. When harnessed effectively, motivation helps us
    reach our own goals and also inspires and influences others
    positively.

4. *Empathy* is the ability to understand and share the feelings
    of others. It allows us to connect more deeply and respond
    effectively to the emotions of those around us. When we
    lack empathy, communication becomes one sided and
    fails to foster trust and rapport. By cultivating empathy,

we can create a supportive and inclusive environment that encourages collaboration and understanding.

5. *Social skills* encompass the ability to build and maintain healthy relationships, communicate effectively, influence others, and work well in teams. These skills are vital in the business context, where creating alliances and achieving shared goals require strong interpersonal connections. Without well-developed social skills, even the most emotionally intelligent individuals may struggle to establish the necessary rapport and trust with their colleagues.

In the business world, effective communication is essential for creating the allies we need to succeed. To truly excel in communication, we must strike a balance among these five elements. When we overemphasize one element of EQ, we can hinder our ability to connect with others and build meaningful, mutually beneficial relationships. For example, if our self-awareness is excessively high, it can overshadow our empathy and self-regulation, making us appear self-centered and unapproachable. Therefore, instead of trying to change who we are, we should focus on adding to ourselves, to bring balance to our interactions.

EQ in Action

Once there was a young executive named Mason who had always prided themselves on their self-awareness. They believed that understanding their own emotions, strengths, and weaknesses was the key to success in their career. While their self-awareness certainly served them well in many aspects of their professional life, it eventually became apparent that it was overpowering their ability to connect with others.

During a team-building retreat, Mason found themselves struggling to engage with their colleagues. They realized that their constant self-analysis and focus on their own emotions prevented them from truly listening and understanding the perspectives of others. It was as if a wall had been erected, isolating them from their team and hindering effective collaboration.

Recognizing this imbalance in their EQ, Mason made a conscious effort to add empathy and self-regulation to their repertoire. They started by actively listening to their colleagues without immediately interjecting their own thoughts or experiences. This allowed them to understand others' emotions and concerns, which created a more supportive and inclusive environment.

Furthermore, Mason began practicing self-regulation by pausing before reacting to situations. Instead of letting their emotions dictate their responses, they took a moment to reflect and choose a more measured and empathetic approach. This newfound ability to manage their emotions not only improved their communication skills but also earned them the trust and respect of their colleagues.

Over time, Mason's efforts paid off. Their colleagues noticed the positive changes in their communication style and became more receptive to their ideas and leadership. With a more balanced EQ, Mason was able to create unbreakable alliances, leading to greater success in their role as a business leader.

This anecdote showcases how someone can discover that their EQ is out of balance and highlights the steps they took to correct it. By recognizing the impact of their excessive self-awareness and actively working on adding empathy and self-regulation to their skill set, they were able to enhance their communication and build stronger relationships in the workplace.

Bringing these five elements of EQ into balance is crucial for enhancing our communication skills and developing unbreakable alliances. By continually assessing ourselves and identifying elements that we may be overemphasizing, we can work on adding to those that need improvement. This approach allows us to enhance our EQ and create an environment where effective communication—and our business endeavors—can thrive.

Overcoming Language Barriers: Strategies for Effective Communication

Throughout my career, I have encountered numerous situations where language differences posed challenges. When faced with language barriers, we need to employ strategies that ensure effective communication and bridge the gap between different languages.

One of the first steps in addressing language barriers is to work with an interpreter or translator. When I was with the FBI, many of the individuals we interacted with did not speak English as their first language. Building a strong relationship with interpreters is crucial as they play a vital role in conveying our messages accurately.

In addition to working with interpreters, I have found that focusing on commonalities is a powerful way to connect with individuals from different language backgrounds. With all of my interactions with Anan, who I discussed earlier, we routinely built upon commonalities of food and fatherhood and eventually established new commonalities together. Regardless of cultural differences, we all share common experiences and interests. By highlighting these shared experiences, such as favorite foods, traditions, or childhood memories, we can establish a sense of familiarity and build a foundation for effective communication.

Nonverbal communication plays a significant role in bypassing language barriers. Regardless of cultural context, nonverbal cues such as body language convey comfort or stress universally. Understanding these cues enables us to gauge the other person's level of comfort and adjust our behavior accordingly. By demonstrating synchronicity in tempo and energy, we show accommodation and create a safe environment for communication to thrive.

Misunderstandings and miscommunications can arise even when language barriers are not present. However, when faced with language differences, it becomes even more important to address and resolve these issues promptly. Taking ownership of our behavior and avoiding defensiveness is crucial in these situations. By accepting responsibility for any miscommunication and avoiding blame or excuses, we establish trust and maintain open lines of communication.

Creating a safe and inclusive environment is paramount when seeking to clarify intentions and resolve misunderstandings. To achieve this, I recommend focusing on the four keys of communication I continue to emphasize. Seek the other person's thoughts and opinions; discuss their priorities, challenges, and pain points; validate their perspective; and empower them with choices. These strategies demonstrate respect, promote open dialogue, and ensure that the other person feels valued and heard.

In today's remote work environment, virtual communication has become the norm. While this presents additional challenges in overcoming language barriers, the principles of rapport building, focusing on commonalities, and attending to nonverbal cues remain just as relevant. By adapting these strategies to the digital realm, we can continue to transcend language barriers and forge strong connections with people worldwide.

Language should never hinder successful collaboration and leadership. These effective communication strategies can help you overcome language barriers, build understanding, and create unbreakable alliances.

Enhancing Virtual Communication for Stronger Relationships

Virtual communications—phone conferences, email, text chats, and especially video calls and conferences—have become the norm for many businesses and organizations. However, this shift presents its own set of challenges when it comes to building and maintaining strong relationships. As a leader, you need to understand these challenges and utilize technology effectively to enhance understanding and connection in these circumstances.

Renowned author and behavioral analysis expert Jack Schafer offers valuable insights into this topic. In his books with co-author Marvin Karlins, *The Like Switch* and *The Truth Detector*, he introduces the concept of "relationship accelerators," which can significantly enhance the strength of alliances in a virtual world. These accelerators serve to forge deeper links with allies and can be used to create meaningful connections even in the absence of face-to-face interactions.[4]

The first and most impactful accelerator is meeting in person. Our genetic and biological makeup is optimized for interpersonal communication to occur in physical proximity. Countless years of evolution have ingrained this need within us. Therefore, when possible, strive to have in-person meetings with your allies, to foster deeper connection and understanding.

If meeting in person is not feasible, the next best option is to use virtual environments where you can see each other. Technologies like Zoom or Google Meet provide the visual element that helps bridge the gap between physical and virtual communication. Seeing the person you are interacting with enhances the overall experience and strengthens your bond.

When visual communication is not possible, hearing each other's voices through phone or conference calls becomes the next best option. While it may not provide the same level of connection as seeing each other, hearing someone's voice adds a personal touch and helps convey emotions more effectively than written communication.

Emails come next in the order of credibility when it comes to virtual communication. Emails grant you the luxury of being more descriptive and detailed, allowing for a deeper understanding of the message you want to convey. Email may lack the personal touch of face-to-face interactions, but it still offers a more substantial connection than shorter forms of communication.

Last, text messaging is the least personalized and shortest form of communication. However, it can be enhanced through the use of emoji. These virtual cues can help display the emotions we are feeling and add context to our words, making our communication more effective and relatable.

While these accelerators provide a framework for enhancing virtual communication, you need to consider additional factors that can further balance the equation. Time and intensity play crucial roles in establishing meaningful connections. If meeting in person is not possible, try to allocate more time for virtual meetings to compensate for the lack of physical presence. Increasing the duration of virtual interactions can help bridge the gap and create a more substantial rapport.

Moreover, the depth and intensity of the conversation also contribute to building stronger relationships. Moving beyond surface-level topics to discuss personal missions, challenges, and pain points can create deeper understanding and nurture empathy. By engaging in meaningful and purposeful conversations, you can overcome the limitations of virtual communication and establish strong alliances.

While virtual communication may never be as effective as face-to-face interactions, numerous techniques and strategies can enhance its impact. By considering the accelerators, as well as factors like proximity, duration, and intensity, you can navigate the virtual landscape and create unbreakable allies. Remember, technology should be viewed less as a barrier to effective communication and more as a tool to enhance understanding and connection.

Ten Actions

1. Practice active listening and show genuine interest in the thoughts and opinions of others. Seek to understand their communication preferences and adapt your delivery style to match their needs.

2. Foster trust and strengthen relationships by actively listening and showing empathy toward others' experiences and emotions. Validate others' thoughts and feelings without judgment.

3. Encourage active participation in conversations by inviting others to share their ideas and opinions. Support them in their decision-making process by offering guidance and allowing them to take ownership of their actions.

4. Practice empathy by actively listening to others, seeking to understand their motivations and needs, and considering their unique context in your interactions.

5. Take time to understand the perspectives of those involved, consider their challenges, and collaborate on finding solutions that meet their needs.

6. Take a step back and empathize with your audience before communicating a message. Consider their concerns, motivations, and aspirations, and frame your message in a way that addresses their needs and aligns with their goals.

7. Familiarize yourself with the four main quadrants of the DISC profile: dominant drivers, influential influencers, steady relators, and conscientious thinkers.

8. Slow down and think before speaking, to allow yourself time to assess the communication style of the person you are interacting with.

9. Tailor the delivery of information to match the person's preferred communication style, which will build better understanding and a stronger alliance.

10. Assess your own communication by recording a conversation and analyzing the congruence between your spoken words and body language. Make adjustments to improve alignment and convey a sense of ease and authenticity.

4

INSPIRE

Moving Beyond Influence and Persuasion

Nothing in life is to be feared, it is only to be understood. Now is the time to understand more, so that we may fear less.
—Marie Curie

Forging Alliances: Inspiring Trust and Protecting National Security

As I sat in the downtown coffee shop, my eyes scanned the room, searching for the individual I'd contacted to meet: a person who held the key to a world of hidden information. Intelligence had reached me about a potential confidential human source, someone with access to valuable insights into the world of espionage. It was my duty to recruit this individual and inspire them to lend their assistance to the FBI's mission of protecting the national security of the United States. My background research on the person revealed that he had deep family roots in serving the country. My hope was that those priorities had transferred to him.

I spotted him sitting alone at a corner table, his demeanor guarded yet curious. Taking a deep breath, I approached him, my heart pounding with anticipation. "Mind if I join you?" I asked, a warm smile playing on my lips.

He looked up, studying me with a mix of caution and intrigue. "Depends on who you are," he replied, his voice tinged with skepticism.

With a genuine tone, I introduced myself as the agent from the Federal Bureau of Investigation who had contacted him about getting together to chat about protecting the nation's security. I assured him that his unique skills and knowledge had not gone unnoticed, and that I believed he had the potential to make a significant impact in the fight against our nation's adversaries, if that was something he might be interested in.

His eyes flickered with curiosity, but his body language remained reserved. "What's in it for me?" he asked, his voice laced with self-preservation.

Leaning in closer, I spoke in hushed tones, my voice filled with earnestness. "Imagine a world where your actions have the power to save lives and bring justice to those who prey on the innocent. A world where you become an integral part of a team that values your expertise and is committed to making a difference."

His skepticism began to wane as I continued. "By sharing your unique insights and connections, you have the ability to expose nefarious intelligence networks and protect the vulnerable. You will play a crucial role in dismantling organizations that thrive on destruction, secrecy, and deceit."

A flicker of purpose sparked in his eyes. He saw the potential to make a genuine impact, to be part of something bigger than himself. He managed to shift his focus from his own reservations to the greater good.

"This is not just about me convincing you to help us," I emphasized in a sincere tone. "It's about offering you an opportunity to be the catalyst for change, to inspire others to take a stand against those who seek to harm our society. If you are willing, we need your unique perspective and expertise to ensure justice prevails."

A smile tugged at the corners of his lips, a glimmer of excitement replacing his initial skepticism. "I want to be a force for good," he said with determination. "Count me in."

And just like that, we had gained a valuable confidential human source, someone who understood the power of inspiration and the importance of focusing on the greater mission. Together, we would forge unbreakable alliances, gather critical intelligence, and protect our nation from those who sought to do harm.

In the realm of espionage and national security, trust and genuine connection are essential. By making it about him, inspiring him to lend his assistance, I offered him partnership on mutual respect and shared goals. The principles outlined earlier in the book had proven their worth once again, guiding us toward success in our mission to protect and serve.

Influence and Persuasion

Although the terms "influence" and "persuasion" are often used inter-changeably, understanding the key differences between them is crucial when it comes to building alliances and creating strong relationships. To truly forge trust and create unbreakable allies, we must dig deep into the meanings of these words and consider where our focus lies.

Let's start by examining Merriam-Webster's definition of influence: "The power or capacity of causing an effect in indirect or intangible ways; the act or power of producing an effect without apparent exertion of force or direct exercise of command; corrupt interference with authority for personal gain."[1] The definition of persuasion is: "to move by argument, entreaty, or expostulation to a belief, position, or course of action." "Influence" has a nuance of being more passive in its efforts and persuasion more aggressive and overt. They are different definitions, but both are focused on you convincing someone else to take action or adopt your way of thinking.

The striking aspect of both influence and persuasion is where the focus lies. If our focus is solely on ourselves, our agenda, and the outcome we desire, we have a high probability of failure. Human beings can sense when someone's intentions are not genuine, and they will disconnect if they feel that their wants, dreams, aspirations, pain points, and challenges are not being acknowledged. Therefore, when we approach building alliances and forging strong relationships, we must shift our focus from thinking about how we can get someone to do something or how we can influence or persuade them, to striving to inspire them.

Inspiration comes from within the other person. It makes them the center of attention. When we become the key that unlocks a solution to one of their problems, offering ourselves as a resource for resolving their challenges and helping them succeed, we inspire them. Inspiration is about them and their needs.

This distinction is critical when it comes to building and forging allies. The focus must always be on the other person.

To create unbreakable allies, you must prioritize inspiration over influence or persuasion. Shift your focus from yourself and your agenda to the other person and their needs. Then watch as trust and strong relationships flourish. Remember, inspiration is the key to success in building alliances.

Strategies for Inspiring Allies: Apply the Keys to Communication

As we explore this topic, it is essential to highlight and understand the four keys to effective communication, which once again will serve as the foundation for our strategies. Using these keys, we can unlock the potential within our allies and become a valuable resource for their success.

The first step in inspiring allies is *discovering their priorities, challenges, and pain points*. By taking the time to understand what drives and concerns them, we can tailor our approach to their specific needs. This requires active listening and empathy, allowing us to gain insight into their journey and the outcomes they desire.

The second key is *communicating in terms of them.* To inspire allies, we must demonstrate genuine curiosity about their path, destination, and desired outcomes. By showing a sincere interest in their goals, we create a connection that develops trust and collaboration. This approach allows us to align our strategies with their aspirations, ensuring that we are working together toward a common goal.

Empowering allies with choice is another critical strategy for inspiring action. When we provide options and choices that align with our own objectives, we give them a sense of ownership and control. This empowers them to take action and actively participate in the alliance. By presenting choices that are mutually beneficial, we strengthen the bond and increase the likelihood of enduring success.

However, strategies alone are not enough to inspire allies. Our behavior also plays a crucial role in maintaining strong relationships. *Communicating openly and honestly* is vital to fostering trust and transparency. By creating an environment where allies feel comfortable sharing their thoughts and concerns, we can address issues proactively and find solutions together.

Demonstrating vulnerability is another essential behavior in inspiring allies. When we show vulnerability, we convey authenticity and build deeper connections. It allows us to relate to others on a human level and encourages them to reciprocate, strengthening the bond of trust and collaboration.

Exhibiting credibility is the final key behavior. By consistently delivering on our promises and demonstrating expertise in our field, we establish ourselves as reliable, trustworthy partners. When allies have confidence in our abilities, they will be more likely to take action and follow our lead.

Example: Emma's Success

In a bustling conference room filled with industry leaders, Emma, a young and ambitious entrepreneur, found herself in a challenging situation. She had just launched her startup and was eager to form alliances with key players in her industry. However, she struggled to capture their attention and inspire their support.

Determined to find a solution, Emma reflected on her recent coaching session with Robin. During their session, Robin shared practical strategies for inspiring allies, emphasizing the importance of understanding their priorities and challenges. He advised Emma to take the time to listen and learn about the path her potential allies were on, the destination they were seeking, and the outcomes they desired.

Armed with this knowledge, Emma attended a networking event where she had the opportunity to meet influential figures in her industry. As she engaged in conversations, she focused on being genuinely curious and nonjudgmental, asking insightful questions about their goals and aspirations. She made a conscious effort to communicate in terms of them, showing a sincere interest in their success.

One particular encounter stood out to Emma. She met Carter, a renowned industry expert who was known for his strategic thinking and influential network. Emma applied the strategy of empowering allies with choice, presenting Carter with options that aligned with her startup's objectives while also considering his own interests. She proposed a collaborative project that would leverage both of their strengths and create mutual benefits.

To Emma's delight, Carter was intrigued by her proposal. He appreciated her understanding of his priorities and the genuine effort she had put into aligning their goals. Impressed by her approach, Carter agreed to form an alliance, confident that together, they could achieve remarkable success.

As Emma's alliance with Carter flourished, she continued to apply the strategies for inspiring allies. One key behavior that Emma embraced was open, honest communication. She cultivated an environment where both she and Carter felt comfortable sharing their thoughts, concerns, and even potential obstacles they might face along the way.

This transparent approach allowed them to address any challenges proactively and find innovative solutions together. They recognized that by openly discussing their ideas and concerns, they could capitalize on their collective strengths and overcome any obstacles that came their way.

In addition to open communication, Emma also demonstrated vulnerability. She shared her own experiences—both successes and failures—with Carter. By doing so, she created an atmosphere of authenticity and trust. Carter reciprocated by sharing his own vulnerabilities, allowing their alliance to deepen further.

Emma's credibility played a crucial role in maintaining the strength of their alliance. She consistently delivered on her promises, which showed her reliability and commitment to their shared goals. Through her dedication and expertise, she earned Carter's respect and trust, cementing their partnership.

Together, Emma and Carter achieved remarkable success through their unbreakable alliance. Their combined efforts and shared vision propelled their businesses to new heights. They celebrated victories together and navigated challenges as a team, always guided by the strategies for inspiring allies that Robin had shared.

Their success story became an inspiration to others in the industry. Emma's dedication to understanding her allies' priorities, communicating in terms of them, empowering them with choices, and exhibiting key behaviors such as open communication, vulnerability, and credibility showcased the transformative power of these strategies.

As word spread about her achievements with Carter, Emma became known as a leader who understood the value of strong alliances and applied practical strategies to inspire others. She also became a sought-after speaker, sharing her experiences and the strategies she had learned, and empowering aspiring entrepreneurs to create their own unbreakable alliances.

Emma's journey exemplifies the effectiveness of the strategies for inspiring allies. She was able to form a strong and unbreakable alliance that propelled her business forward. Her success testifies to the transformative power of these strategies and the potential they hold for leaders in any industry.

To summarize, the strategies for inspiring allies involve discovering their priorities, challenges, and pain points; communicating in terms of them; empowering them with choices that align with our goals; and exhibiting key behaviors such as open communication, vulnerability, and credibility. By implementing these strategies and adopting the right mindset, we can create unbreakable alliances that lead to mutual success.

Building Organic Alignment: Fostering Genuine Allies with Shared Goals and Values

In the pursuit of success and creating unbreakable alliances, it is crucial to establish a solid foundation of shared goals and values with our allies. However, genuine alignment cannot be forced or contrived; it must be cultivated organically. By recognizing the importance of ensuring our interests align with those of our allies, we can create a win–win situation without compromising our own objectives.

Forcing a situation that lacks organic alignment will only result in unwilling accomplices rather than willing allies. Just as in the realm of confidential human-source recruitment, the number of sources is not as significant as their quality. It is far more effective to have a few allies who wholeheartedly contribute to the alliance than to have a larger number who reluctantly offer minimal effort.

To achieve this alignment, we need to be transparent and clear about our intentions. By removing any hidden agendas or deceptive tactics, we empower our allies to make informed choices. Encouraging them to ask questions and seek clarification ensures that they fully understand our goals and objectives. This level of transparency fosters trust and establishes a solid foundation for collaboration.

In building genuine alliances, it is important to recognize incongruities early on. If our goals and values do not align with those of our potential allies, it may be necessary to gracefully move on without harboring hard feelings. This allows us to focus our efforts on cultivating relationships that have the potential for long-term success.

In our approach to achieving alignment, we must remember that inspiration is far more powerful than coercion. Instead of trying to convince others to align with our objectives, we should strive to inspire them by showcasing the benefits and opportunities that arise from the alliance. By presenting our proposition as a service, we demonstrate a commitment to a greater purpose and emphasize the mutual benefits that can be derived from the partnership.

As noted, it is better to have a few dedicated allies who are genuinely invested in the alliance than a multitude of hesitant partners. These true allies become beacons of support, further enhancing our reputation and building a positive brand. Even if someone initially lacks interest in becoming an ally, maintaining a respectful and positive relationship with them can open doors for future opportunities.

Building organic alignment is essential for developing genuine allies with shared goals and values. By prioritizing transparency, empowering others with choice, and offering service rather than manipulation, we can establish strong and mutually beneficial relationships that lead to ongoing success. In this way, we create unbreakable alliances that propel us toward our collective goals.

Balancing Ethics and Persuasion for Successful Alliances

In the world of business leadership, the desire to persuade others and achieve our goals often clashes with the need to respect their individual autonomy and free will. How do we navigate this delicate balance? How can we ethically influence others without compromising their autonomy? These questions lie at the heart of successful alliances and effective leadership. Words can be full of nuance, and I remain a greater fan of the word "inspire" as compared to "persuade" and "influence" for the reasons stated earlier, but I do recognize that the latter are common words and often well intentioned. Let's take a look at how we can use them ethically.

When it comes to ethics and persuasion, I believe they can go hand in hand if we approach them with transparency and consideration for others. Having a clear agenda and objectives is crucial, but equally important is sharing that agenda openly with those we seek to persuade. By being transparent, we inspire trust and establish a foundation of honesty and openness.

Let's consider a situation where this balance is essential. Imagine you are working under a strict deadline set by your boss or organization. You need to persuade someone to move faster, but you don't want to manipulate or coerce them. In such cases, you must communicate your timeline openly and honestly. Tell them about your deadline and acknowledge their autonomy in deciding whether they can accommodate it. By doing so, you show respect for their time and preferences, and you maintain a healthy relationship based on trust and understanding.

Ethics, to me, is all about transparency. It means being up front about your intentions, needs, and limitations. It means avoiding manipulation and hidden agendas. In my experience, transparency has been the key to building strong alliances and maintaining a positive dialogue with others.

Interestingly, this perspective on ethics comes from someone who had to navigate the gray line between right and wrong during my time in the FBI. Working in counterintelligence and recruiting confidential human sources required innovative thinking and constantly staying ahead of adversaries. In such situations, there were no established policies or procedures to guide us. We had to rely on outside-the-box thinking and adaptability.

To ensure ethical decision making, I relied on the concept of a "loving critic": someone who acts as a sounding board, providing objective feedback on our actions and decisions without the emotional attachment we may have to the outcome. They are people with whom we can be open and honest when seeking their perspective. They care deeply for us but are not swayed by our justifications. This allows them to provide valuable insights and keep us grounded.

During my time in the FBI, I often bounced ideas off a trusted friend or colleague on the squad. If I hesitated to share my plans with my supervisor or others who had more experience, it served as a gut check—it was a sign that my actions might not align with ethical principles. This practice of seeking feedback from ethical loving critics helped me maintain a high standard of ethics in my work.

Balancing ethics and persuasion is essential for creating unbreakable alliances and achieving success in business leadership. It requires transparency, open communication, and a willingness to seek feedback from ethical loving critics. By respecting others' autonomy and being honest about our intentions, we can build trust and foster productive relationships that stand the test of time.

Embracing Diversity and Inclusion: A Thought Experiment

When pursuing diversity and inclusion, we often find ourselves caught up in our own behaviors, unaware of their possible impact on others. It is a fascinating challenge, one that requires us to look beyond our own perspectives and truly understand the experiences and backgrounds of those we interact with.

As both theoretical physicist Albert Einstein and astrophysicist Neil deGrasse Tyson have shown us, empathy plays a crucial role in this process. When encountering someone new, someone whose life arc is unfamiliar to us, we must approach them with curiosity and an open mind.[2]

Diversity and inclusion are about discovering the life arc of another individual—understanding what has shaped them, what experiences and influences have contributed to their identity today. By taking the time to uncover their story without judgment, we pave the way for true diversity and inclusion.

Ultimately, everyone seeks to feel valued and seen. The key to achieving this lies in curiosity. Be present and genuinely curious about others. Ask questions, seek to understand, and listen actively. By doing so, we create an environment where people feel acknowledged and appreciated.

To further enhance our ability to embrace diversity and inclusion, we can engage in a thought experiment. This involves putting ourselves in the shoes of the person we are communicating with. Imagine receiving the message from their perspective, considering their life arc and experiences. How would it look? How would it feel? By reversing our roles in this way, we gain valuable insights into how others may perceive our words and actions.

In my previous work with intelligence operations, we often employed this thought experiment to strategize recruitment efforts. We would role-play as the target individual, immersing ourselves in their daily routine, challenges, and stresses. This allowed us to craft a plan that would truly resonate with them, rather than one that simply sounded good to us.

By practicing this thought experiment in our own lives, we can develop a deeper understanding of others and their perspectives. We can approach diversity and inclusion with empathy and authenticity, creating an environment where everyone feels heard and valued. Let us therefore embrace the challenge of diversity and inclusion, and set forth on this thought-provoking journey of self-reflection and critical thinking.

A Sample Thought Experiment

Let's consider a scenario where a company is implementing a new diversity and inclusion initiative. The CEO gathers the leadership team to discuss how to approach this initiative effectively. One of the team members suggests hosting a diversity training workshop for all employees, believing that it will address any biases and prejudices that may exist within the organization.

However, in the spirit of the thought experiment, the CEO encourages the team to consider the perspective of the employees who will be attending the workshop. They ask the team to imagine being in the shoes of those employees—people from various backgrounds, with different experiences, and unique life arcs.

The team then starts to think about the potential impact of the workshop from the employees' point of view. They consider the format, the content, and the delivery of the training. They ask themselves questions such as, will the employees feel engaged and valued during the workshop? Will they see it as a genuine effort to promote inclusivity, or will it come across as a mere checkbox exercise? How can we ensure that the training addresses their specific concerns and challenges?

As they delve deeper into the thought experiment, the team realizes that a one-size-fits-all approach may not be the most effective solution. Instead, they propose a more personalized format, where employees are given the opportunity to share their own experiences and perspectives in a safe and supportive environment. This way, the training becomes a platform for dialogue, understanding, and growth.

By conducting this thought experiment, the leadership team gains a deeper understanding of the employees' needs and concerns. They recognize that true diversity and inclusion require more than just a one-time workshop; they require ongoing efforts to create a culture where everyone feels valued and heard.

As a result, the CEO decides to incorporate employee feedback and suggestions into the diversity and inclusion initiative. The company establishes employee resource groups, provides mentorship opportunities, and encourages open conversations about diversity and inclusion throughout the organization. This approach ensures that biases and prejudices are actively addressed and inclusivity becomes an integral part of the company's DNA.

Through the power of thought experiments and empathetic thinking, the organization takes a significant step toward creating an inclusive and diverse workplace, where every employee feels respected, valued, and included.

Tailoring Your Approach

Tailoring your approach to different audiences is crucial for effective communication and gaining buy-in for your ideas. It requires doing your homework and understanding your audience's goals, objectives, and desired outcomes. By knowing their "big, overarching why," you can frame your message in a way that resonates with them.

If you have the opportunity to prepare ahead of time, make sure to research your audience and gather as much information as possible. This will help you develop a plan that you believe will be effective. However, even with extensive preparation, you might still be off the mark. That's when an impromptu needs assessment becomes invaluable.

When giving a keynote speech or workshop, start by asking your audience what they think the great outcome should be for the session. This question not only engages them but also gives you insights into their expectations and desired takeaways. By involving them in the process, you create a sense of ownership and make them feel heard.

An impromptu needs assessment allows you to tailor your content in real time. Since you have mastered your material beforehand, you can confidently adjust your delivery to meet their specific needs. This flexibility demonstrates your adaptability and shows that you are invested in their success.

Additionally, pay attention to nonverbal cues when presenting your ideas. Watch, listen, and gauge how your audience is reacting. Are they engaged and comfortable, or do they show signs of stress or disinterest? If you notice any indications of unease or disengagement, address them immediately. Ask if you are on the right track, if they need further explanations, or if they prefer to explore a different path. Creating an environment where your audience feels comfortable providing feedback is essential.

Timing is crucial when addressing potential concerns or seeking feedback. Choose a moment when it is appropriate, such as during a break or in a more private setting. By addressing any issues proactively, you can keep your audience engaged and ensure that your message is effectively communicated.

In summary, tailoring your approach to different audiences requires thorough preparation, active listening, and flexibility. By doing your homework, conducting impromptu needs assessments, and paying attention to nonverbal cues, you can adapt your communication style to meet your audience's specific needs. This personalized approach enhances your credibility and authority while fostering stronger alliances and increasing the likelihood of success.

Crafting Compelling Narratives

In the realm of business leadership, storytelling holds a remarkable power to capture attention, engage allies, and ultimately achieve success. As a leader, I have witnessed firsthand the transformative impact of storytelling in forging unbreakable alliances.

Randy Olson's book *The Narrative Gym*, which has proven to be an invaluable tool in my journey as a leader, provides a three-sentence strategy. This approach, known as the "and, but, therefore" statement, presents a challenge, offers a potential solution, and highlights the path to overcoming that challenge. By employing this structure, such as in the following example, I have been able to seize the

attention of my audience and maintain their engagement throughout the storytelling process:

> In the fast-paced world of technology, businesses are constantly seek-
> ing innovative solutions to streamline their operations *and* enhance
> efficiency.
>
> *But*, ever-increasing cyber-threats pose a significant challenge to
> safeguarding sensitive data and maintaining secure networks.
>
> *Therefore*, implementing state-of-the-art cybersecurity measures
> becomes paramount to protect valuable assets, maintain customer
> trust, and ensure uninterrupted business operations.[3]

Beyond the Gym

To begin crafting a narrative, you must establish a strong introduc-
tion that sets the stage for the main characters, themes, and problems at hand. This initial context allows allies to personally connect
with the story and understand its significance. As you unfold the narrative, incorporate rising action, employing compelling anecdotes or
real-life experiences to build tension and sustain interest.

The climax of the story is a pivotal moment where you unveil
the solution to the challenge. This turning point captivates allies and
demonstrates the efficacy of the proposed solution. Following the
climax, present a resolution that outlines the implementation of the
solution and the subsequent outcome. It is imperative that you tailor
the storytelling format to the specific audience, taking into account
their interests, values, and preferences.

Relatable characters and situations play a vital role in making a narrative compelling. By infusing relatable elements, leaders can ensure that allies connect with the story on an emotional level. Such engagement becomes a powerful catalyst for persuading allies to join the cause and wholeheartedly commit to the proposed solution.

To illustrate the potency of storytelling, I often share personal stories from my own life experiences. For instance, I reflect on my humble background, growing up in a financially challenged environment where we relied on chopping wood to heat our home. This formative experience instilled resilience and self-reliance within me, but it also revealed my self-focused nature, hindering my ability to truly lead.

Through these personal stories, I convey the importance of shifting focus from self to others. I highlight the significance of the four keys of communication: seeking thoughts and opinions, speaking in terms of others' priorities, validating them, and empowering them with choices. These skills have propelled me forward in my leadership roles while proving instrumental in recruiting spies, being part of the team at Parris Island, South Carolina, that created the Crucible for the Marine Corps, writing books, and delivering inspirational speeches.

By mastering the art of crafting compelling narratives, leaders can navigate the intricate terrain of business leadership, forging unbreakable alliances that pave the way to unprecedented success.

Leveraging Emotional Intelligence for Persuasion and Inspiration

EQ plays a pivotal role in connecting with others, whether it is to persuade or inspire them. Let's explore how to leverage the five elements of EQ: self-awareness, self-regulation, motivation, empathy, and social skills—to appeal to the emotions of others in a persuasive and inspirational manner.

To begin with, *self-awareness* is crucial when presenting our ideas and connecting with an audience. Keeping our focus on the audience rather than ourselves is important. One effective strategy is to eliminate the use of "I" statements and instead use "we" and "you" statements. By doing so, the focus shifts to the listener, making them feel acknowledged and valued.

Self-regulation is the next element of EQ that we must harness. Maintaining emotional balance is vital when engaging with others. People are more likely to connect with us when they witness our ability to handle situations with composure and control. This doesn't mean suppressing our emotions, but rather expressing them in a healthy and constructive manner.

High motivation and energy are desirable traits when appealing to others. However, it is important to channel these qualities in a controlled manner, ensuring that we do not lose control of ourselves. By exhibiting enthusiasm and passion while remaining composed, we create an environment where others feel motivated and inspired to take action.

Empathy, the ability to understand and relate to others, is a powerful tool in appealing to emotions. By putting ourselves in the shoes of our audience, we can better understand their needs, desires, and concerns. It allows us to deliver our message in a way that resonates with them, rather than imposing our own agenda. This empathetic approach ensures that we give people what they want, in the way they want to receive it.

Last, *social skills* play a crucial role in connecting with an audience before, during, and after any interaction. Building relationships and establishing a personal reputation and brand are essential for effective communication. Engaging with individuals beforehand, be it in a casual setting or a professional environment, helps create a foundation of trust and familiarity. This, in turn, paves the way for a more meaningful and impactful connection when the time comes to present our ideas.

History has presented countless examples of individuals who have mastered the art of leveraging EQ to appeal to others' emotions in a persuasive and inspirational manner. Leaders like Martin Luther King Jr. tapped into the emotions of millions with his iconic "I Have a Dream" speech, inspiring them to fight for equality and justice. By expressing empathy, understanding, and unwavering conviction, he created an unbreakable bond with his audience.

In the business world, Steve Jobs was renowned for his ability to connect with customers and employees alike. By understanding their desires and aspirations, he created products and experiences that not only met their needs but also touched them on an emotional level. Jobs's persuasive and inspirational communication style was rooted in his keen EQ, allowing him to build a fiercely loyal customer base and a motivated workforce.

These examples highlight the power of EQ in appealing to others' emotions. By honing our self-awareness, self-regulation, motivation, empathy, and social skills, we can create unbreakable alliances with those around us. Whether it is to persuade stakeholders, inspire a team, or connect with customers, EQ is the compass that guides us toward success.

Mastering the Art of Persuasive and Inspirational Presentations

As we have learned throughout this book, building successful alliances requires effective communication and the ability to influence and inspire others positively. Whether you are pitching a new business idea, motivating your team, or seeking support for your vision, your presentation skills can make all the difference in achieving your desired outcomes. So, let's explore the key takeaways and practical exercises to help you become a master presenter.

Repetition: The Key to Mastery

As the saying goes, "Everything in life comes down to reps." Just like any other skill, presenting ideas effectively requires practice and repetition. The more you engage in presenting, the better you become at connecting with your audience, conveying your message, and achieving your desired outcomes. Don't shy away from opportunities to present, whether it's in team meetings, conferences, or even informal gatherings. Embrace every chance to refine your presentation skills and gain valuable experience.

Know Your Audience

Before crafting your presentation, take the time to understand your audience. What are their needs, concerns, and interests? Tailor your message to resonate with them by addressing their specific pain points and offering solutions. By demonstrating that you understand their unique challenges, you establish trust and credibility, making your ideas more compelling and persuasive.

Storytelling: The Power of Emotion

One of the most effective ways to captivate your audience is through storytelling. Humans are hardwired to connect with stories that evoke emotions. Craft your presentation as a narrative that engages your audience's imagination and stirs their feelings. Use real-life examples, anecdotes, or personal experiences to illustrate your points and make your ideas relatable. By appealing to the heart, you create a lasting impact that inspires action.

Visual Aids and Multimedia

In today's digital age, visual aids and multimedia have become indispensable tools for impactful presentations. Incorporate relevant images, videos, charts, or graphs that support your ideas and enhance understanding. Visual cues make your presentation more appealing while helping viewers retain information. However, remember to strike a balance—your visuals should supplement your message, not overshadow it.

Engage and Involve Your Audience

A compelling presentation is not a monologue; it's an interactive experience. Engage your audience by asking thought-provoking questions, encouraging participation, and creating space for discussions. Incorporate activities or exercises that require audience involvement, which will foster a sense of ownership and investment in your ideas. By making your audience an active part of the presentation, you heighten their engagement and increase the likelihood of persuasion.

Practice Active Listening

To be persuasive, you must be receptive to your audience's feedback and concerns. Practice active listening throughout your presentation by observing nonverbal cues, responding empathetically, and addressing any doubts or objections raised. By demonstrating that you value their input and are genuinely interested in their perspectives, you create an atmosphere of trust and collaboration, making your ideas more compelling and persuasive.

Becoming a master presenter requires dedication, practice, and a genuine desire to connect with and inspire others. By following the techniques and strategies outlined in this section, you can elevate your presentation skills and create unbreakable alliances. Remember, every opportunity to present is a chance to refine your craft and make a lasting impact.

Ten Actions

1. Focus on inspiring others by shifting your focus from yourself to the other person and offering solutions to their specific needs.
2. Avoid manipulation and prioritize genuine inspiration that comes from within the other person.
3. Prioritize trust and effective communication in building and maintaining alliances.

4. Discover allies' priorities and challenges through active listening and empathy.

5. Communicate in terms of your allies' goals and aspirations to create a connection based on trust and collaboration.

6. Empower allies with choices to increase engagement and collaboration.

7. Cultivate organic alignment by establishing shared goals and values through transparent communication.

8. Elevate quality over quantity in alliances by investing in relationships with dedicated and aligned allies.

9. Approach diversity and inclusion with curiosity and empathy, conducting thought experiments and implementing personalized initiatives.

10. Tailor your approach by conducting research on your audience, using impromptu needs assessments, and paying attention to nonverbal cues.

5

OWN IT

Resolving Conflicts
Through Your Actions

A person who never made a mistake never tried anything new.
—Albert Einstein

Navigating Conflicts: The Power of
Collaboration and Mindful Leadership

Some time ago, I found myself leading a highly skilled and diverse behavioral team, tasked with a top-secret spy recruitment operation. Each team member brought their unique expertise and perspective to the table, but as we explored the details, it became apparent that we differed on how to proceed.

On one side, Agent Ramirez (all agents' names pseudonymous), with her bold and assertive approach, advocated for a direct, aggressive recruitment strategy. She believed that we should actively seek out potential confidential human sources to aid the operation, approach them head-on, and persuade them to join our cause.

On the other side, Agent Chen, known for her strategic thinking and subtlety, proposed a more open and patient approach. She argued that we should observe potential sources discreetly over time, gather intel on their motivations and priorities, and then make a calculated approach when the time was right for them.

The tension in the room was palpable. It seemed as if the mission would be compromised if we couldn't find common ground. As the team leader, I was responsible for guiding us toward resolution and ensuring the success of the operation.

With a deep breath, I decided to address the conflicting opinions. I wanted to create an environment where open dialogue and collaboration could flourish. The room buzzed with anticipation as we gathered, ready to debate and find a way forward.

I kicked off the discussion by acknowledging each team member's expertise and value. I emphasized that our goal was to recruit the best confidential human sources for the operation while maintaining the utmost secrecy and integrity.

Listening intently, I let Ramirez and Chen present their thoughts, giving them the floor to express their reasoning and perspectives. The room grew animated as they passionately defended their approaches, each convinced that theirs was the superior strategy.

As I observed the heated debate, a sudden realization struck me. Despite their differing methods, both Ramirez and Chen shared the same underlying recruitment goal I had just laid out. Their approaches were two sides of the same coin, each with its own merits and potential pitfalls.

With this newfound understanding, I guided the conversation toward finding common ground. We discussed the advantages and challenges of each approach, dissecting the potential risks and rewards. Together, we brainstormed a hybrid strategy that combined elements of both direct recruitment and patient observation.

Excitement filled the room as ideas flowed freely. We forged a path that allowed us to leverage the strengths of each approach, striking a delicate balance between assertiveness and subtlety. It was a strategy that maximized our chances of recruiting top-tier sources while minimizing the risk of exposure and overplaying our hand.

As the meeting concluded, a sense of unity and shared purpose permeated the air. We had transformed our initial conflict into a catalyst for innovation. The meeting ended with a newfound understanding and respect for each other's perspectives.

In the weeks that followed, we implemented our hybrid strategy with precision and finesse. Our recruitment operation proved to be a resounding success, attracting talented and dedicated spies to our cause. Not only did the mission's triumph solidify our team's reputation, it also cemented the unbreakable bonds forged through our conflict resolution process.

This thrilling experience taught me the power of open dialogue, collaboration, and finding common ground. It showed me that conflicts, when approached with respect and a shared goal, can lead to extraordinary outcomes. By embracing diverse perspectives and valuing the expertise of each team member, we can navigate even the most complex challenges and achieve unparalleled success.

Conflict resolution is a vital skill for any leader. But before we dive into the best techniques and strategies, let's start with a simple understanding: the best way to resolve a conflict is not to have one in the first place. How can we achieve that? By adopting the mindset and behaviors of someone who doesn't create conflict.

We've all heard the old cliché that to lead others, you must first lead yourself. Similarly, to resolve conflict with others, you must first resolve conflict within yourself. In most situations, where does conflict come from? It stems from ego, vanity, insecurities, and a battle of wills against others because we feel slighted or disenfranchised. Conflict arises when we emotionally react to the world and the stimuli around us, based not just on our genetics and biology but also on the experiences that have shaped our lives.

The key to resolving conflicts lies in maintaining a cognitive, thoughtful process. Many of the behaviors and skills required for conflict resolution can be found within Stoicism. Stoicism provides a strategy for solving challenges, reframing conflict as simply another emotional response to a challenge. As leaders, it is our duty to work and solve problems and challenges. Conflict is just a fancy word for a struggle or disagreement between two or more parties with opposing interests.

Creating allies is all about aligning the "why." In conflict resolution, it is important to prioritize the relationship and the ally over the material outcome you seek. Sometimes, to maintain the relationship, you may have to let go of that outcome. Strange as it may sound, placing the ally, the relationship, and the trust you share above the momentary disagreement will ultimately lead to a better outcome.

Another aspect of resolving conflicts is understanding context. We often unintentionally disregard others' context. We fail to acknowledge that the other person has put in as much time, effort, and energy into their decision-making process as we have. If they come up with a solution or a way to execute something that we don't agree with, we need to get curious and nonjudgmentally explore their perspective. Letting go of our biases and approaching conflicts with curiosity can be a powerful method for resolving and preventing them.

In my experience, I have found that conflicts are becoming increasingly rare. Yes, there are disagreements from time to time, as we all have emotional flare-ups when things don't go our way or disrupt our routine. However, when conflicts arise, the key is to focus on what you *can* control: your own behavior. Ask yourself, "What did I do to make them feel unsafe with this decision?" Taking ownership of your role in the conflict and understanding that the other party may not feel secure with your proposed approach is the first step in resolving conflicts.

By adopting a thoughtful process and understanding the underlying behaviors that drive conflicts, we can make current conflicts disappear and prevent future ones. This is the mindset we must adopt for effective conflict resolution.

Understanding Different Viewpoints: A Path to Resolving Conflicts Within Alliances

Conflicts within alliances are inevitable, especially when working closely with allies for an extended period of time. In my career, I have encountered numerous conflicts within alliances, particularly during my time at the FBI. Collaborating with colleagues and forming alliances is a crucial aspect of our work in counterintelligence and protecting the national security of the United States.

Allow me to share an illuminating example of a conflict within an alliance that I was asked to resolve after my retirement.

The scenario involved a squad that had been diligently working on a recruitment operation for a high-level intelligence officer. They had devised an excellent plan and had been preparing for this operation for years. However, one of their team members had recently been promoted and was now overseeing the operation from FBI headquarters, where strategic decisions were made. To their dismay, their trusted ally at headquarters denied their operation.

When I arrived at the office, the team was frustrated and upset, badmouthing their former ally. Instead of jumping into strategizing another recruitment operation, I decided to approach the situation by understanding different viewpoints and employing the techniques that I have developed over the years.

I started by asking the team a series of questions to shift their perspective. I inquired if they enjoyed their current work, lifestyle, and sense of safety. They confirmed that they were satisfied with their present situation and felt secure. I then asked them if the failure of this particular operation would significantly affect any of these aspects of their lives. They admitted that it wouldn't, as they would simply move on to another operation. They would still be safe and continue their work regardless.

Next, I prompted them to consider their ally who had taken the promotion to headquarters. I asked them to speculate about his main priorities now that he was in an executive leadership position. It became apparent that their former ally's primary goal was to eventually leave headquarters and return to the field with a promotion to the position of squad supervisor, where he could execute missions at a more strategic level. I emphasized that his focus had shifted from the tactical level of individual operations to the strategic level of advancing his career.

By reframing the situation and considering their former ally's perspective, the team began to understand that their actions and communication had inadvertently made him feel unsafe about moving forward with the operation. They had disregarded his follow-up questions and failed to address his concerns adequately. I urged them to think about what they could do to make him feel safe and confident in supporting their plans.

Instead of trying to win the argument or come up with clever strategies, I emphasized the importance of simplifying the approach. The key was to genuinely listen to their ally's needs and concerns and find ways to address them effectively. I encouraged the team to apologize for their behavior, seek his thoughts and opinions, and validate his concerns. They did just that, and through open and respectful communication, they were able to reach a compromise that accommodated his new context and needs.

Ultimately, the conflict was resolved, and they erased the fact that they even had one. By understanding different viewpoints, owning their behavior, and making their ally feel safe, they successfully navigated the conflict and maintained a strong alliance.

Understanding different viewpoints is a crucial skill when conflicts arise within alliances. It requires consuming the same information as your ally, gaining knowledge, and developing a deeper understanding of your ally's experiences. This gives you a significant advantage in communication while helping them feel heard and supported in reaching a resolution.

Conflicts within alliances are opportunities for growth and strengthening relationships. By approaching these conflicts with empathy, a willingness to understand different viewpoints, and a commitment to making allies feel safe, we can resolve conflicts effectively and create unbreakable alliances.

Ego: The Enemy of Conflict Resolution and Unbreakable Alliances

In the realm of conflict resolution and building unbreakable alliances, ego can be our greatest adversary. As Ryan Holiday explores in his book *Ego Is the Enemy*, an unhealthy belief in our own importance and a sense of superiority can hinder our ability to resolve conflicts effectively and maintain strong alliances. To truly achieve success in this area, we must cultivate humility, self-awareness, and a willingness to learn from others.[1]

Conflict resolution requires us to think less of ourselves and be less invested in the story we tell of ourselves. When ego takes over, we become separated from everything and lose sight of the larger goal of resolving conflicts and building lasting alliances. Ego stifles creativity and prevents us from considering alternative perspectives and solutions. It blinds us to the needs and perspectives of others, making it nearly impossible to build trust and collaboration.

In conflict resolution, it is essential to evaluate our own abilities honestly and avoid being driven solely by ego. We must be willing to accept our own limitations and seek continuous growth and improvement. This self-awareness enables us to approach conflicts with a clear mind and a willingness to listen and understand.

To overcome ego and foster effective conflict resolution, we must become students of the process. By humbly seeking knowledge and guidance from others, we open ourselves up to new perspectives and ideas. Being a student places our ego and ambition in someone else's hands, allowing us to absorb and observe, filter information, and remain self-critical and motivated.

Passion, though often seen as a positive trait, can actually hinder conflict resolution. It can distract us from our weaknesses and the underlying issues at hand. Instead, we should focus on clarity, purpose, and perseverance. By maintaining control and not becoming a slave to passion, we can approach conflicts with a level-headed and deliberate mindset, increasing our chances of finding effective resolutions.

The canvas strategy is a powerful approach to conflict resolution. It involves providing support and clearing a path for others to be their best selves. Think of the strategy as if you are an artist who finds canvases other people can paint on. Your goal is clearing the obstacles for the people around you to be successful artists themselves. By creating paths of success for others, you ultimately create a path of success for yourself. By focusing on helping others succeed, we ultimately create an environment of collaboration and trust, leading to unbreakable alliances. This strategy requires us to restrain ourselves from seeking personal glory and to prioritize the success and well-being of others.[2]

Restraint is another critical skill in conflict resolution. We must resist the urge to undermine our own legacy and instead focus on the task at hand. Ego-driven actions can escalate conflicts and damage relationships, making it difficult to find resolutions. By getting out of our own heads and avoiding feasting on our own thoughts, we can approach conflicts with a clear and open mind.

Pride, too, poses a significant challenge in conflict resolution. It can be a distraction and diluter, hindering our ability to empathize and find common ground. To lead effectively in conflict resolution, we must swallow our pride and remain humble. This allows us to consider perspectives and solutions we otherwise might have overlooked.

In the pursuit of resolving conflicts and building unbreakable alliances, hard work is essential. Reputations are not built on what we plan to do but on the tremendous effort we put into finding resolutions and maintaining strong relationships. Ego is the enemy of this hard work, as it can lead to a sense of entitlement, control, and paranoia that undermines the collaborative process.[3]

As we navigate conflicts and seek to build unbreakable alliances, we must continually remind ourselves to stay humble, maintain our sense of purpose, and avoid the undisciplined pursuit of more. Failure and setbacks are inevitable, but through humility and resilience, we can find the strength to overcome them. By keeping our ego in check and embracing a selfless approach, we can resolve conflicts effectively and create unbreakable alliances that stand the test of time.

The Path to Conflict Resolution: Embracing Self-Leadership and Compassionate Service

In the pursuit of seeking common ground and finding mutually beneficial solutions during conflicts, I often draw inspiration from Robin Sharma's book, *The Monk Who Sold His Ferrari*. In this profound work,

Sharma shares valuable insights and techniques that can guide us in our quest for effective leadership and personal growth.[4]

One of the book's key principles that I embrace is the concept of self-leadership. Sharma emphasizes that those who take the time to strengthen themselves are the strongest. This resonates deeply with me because it highlights the importance of self-awareness and personal development. By constantly improving ourselves, we can approach conflicts with a calm and composed demeanor, allowing us to seek common ground and find mutually beneficial solutions.[5]

Another powerful lesson I've learned from *The Monk Who Sold His Ferrari* is the significance of serving others. Sharma encourages us to use our material bodies with our spiritual passion in the service of others. This mindset shift is crucial when it comes to resolving conflicts. Instead of focusing solely on our own needs and desires, we should strive to understand and empathize with others' perspectives. By actively seeking to serve and help others, we create an environment that encourages collaboration and the discovery of mutually beneficial solutions.[6]

Furthermore, Sharma's book teaches us the importance of mindfulness and self-reflection. He reminds us to approach every interaction and conversation as a great science experiment. This mindset allows us to detach ourselves from the emotions and biases that often cloud our judgment during conflicts. By treating every conflict as an opportunity to learn and grow, we can approach it with curiosity and open-mindedness, seeking common ground and finding innovative solutions.[7]

In my experience, conflicts often arise due to emotional reactions and a sense of feeling slighted. However, as Sharma points out, most of the time these emotions have nothing to do with the actual conflict at hand. Therefore, it is crucial to focus on the process, objectives, and methods involved. By keeping our attention on these aspects, we can navigate conflicts with a clear and rational mindset.[8]

Last, I believe in the power of kindness and compassion in resolving conflicts. Sharma's book reminds us to perform acts of kindness and service every day. This simple practice can have a profound impact on our relationships and the conflicts we encounter. By approaching conflicts with a genuine desire to understand and help others, we create an atmosphere of trust and collaboration. This paves the way for finding mutually beneficial solutions that satisfy the needs and desires of all parties involved.[9]

Seeking common ground and finding mutually beneficial solutions during conflicts requires a combination of self-leadership, service to others, mindfulness, and kindness. By embracing these principles, we can navigate conflicts with grace and effectiveness, ultimately creating unbreakable alliances and succeeding in our endeavors.

Mastering Emotions During Conflict for Effective Leadership

In the tumultuous world of business, conflicts are an inevitable part of leadership. The ability to manage emotions and maintain a composed demeanor during these conflicts is a crucial skill for effective leadership.

As Ryan Holiday shares in his book, *Stillness Is the Key*, inner stillness serves as the cornerstone for managing emotions during conflict. By cultivating a sense of calm and composure, leaders can navigate through conflicts with clarity and make rational decisions.

While conflicts can stir up intense emotions for leaders, what truly matters is how they respond to these emotions.[10]

The first step in managing emotions during conflict is to become aware of them. Leaders must acknowledge and understand their own emotional responses before attempting to address the conflict at hand. This self-awareness allows leaders to separate their emotions from the situation, enabling them to respond more objectively and effectively.

Silence becomes a powerful tool in conflict management. Instead of reacting impulsively, leaders should take a moment to pause and collect their thoughts. This moment of silence allows them to regain control over their emotions and respond in a thoughtful and strategic manner. By using silence as a strategic pause, leaders can defuse tension and create space for constructive dialogue.

Leaders must also seek to understand the emotions of others involved in the conflict. Empathetically listening and acknowledging the emotions of those affected allows leaders to build trust and create an environment conducive to conflict resolution. This requires leaders to put themselves in the shoes of others and validate their feelings, even if they do not agree with them.

A key aspect of managing emotions during conflict is maintaining a sense of perspective. Leaders must remind themselves of the bigger picture and the long-term goals of the organization. This perspective helps them avoid getting caught up in the heat of the moment and losing sight of the objective. By staying focused, leaders can guide the conflict toward a resolution that aligns with the organization's vision.

Another technique for managing emotions during conflict is practicing active listening. Leaders must truly listen to the concerns and perspectives of all parties involved without interrupting or dismissing their viewpoints. Active listening not only demonstrates respect but also allows leaders to gain valuable insights and develop a more comprehensive understanding of the conflict.

Furthermore, leaders should cultivate EQ, which involves recognizing and managing their own emotions as well as understanding the emotions of others. EQ enables leaders to respond to conflicts with empathy and compassion, nurturing an environment of understanding and collaboration. By harnessing EQ, leaders can effectively navigate through conflicts and build stronger relationships with their team members.

Leaders must remember that conflicts are not personal attacks, but rather opportunities for growth and improvement. By reframing conflicts as learning experiences, leaders can approach them with a growth mindset. This perspective allows leaders to detach themselves from negative emotions and focus on finding solutions and fostering positive outcomes.

Mastering emotions during conflict is an essential skill for effective leadership. By cultivating inner stillness, practicing active listening, and developing EQ, leaders can navigate through conflicts with grace and authority. Approaching conflicts with a calm and composed demeanor can help leaders develop an environment of trust, collaboration, and growth within their organizations.

Understanding the Laws of Human Nature

Let's explore the importance of understanding human nature for achieving conflict resolution and establishing unbreakable alliances.

These insights are derived from my own experiences as well as the wisdom shared by Robert Greene in his book *The Laws of Human Nature*.[11]

You may believe that you are a rational individual, capable of making logical decisions. However, the truth is that our rationality is often clouded by biases and emotions. To become more rational, we must follow three essential steps. The first step is to identify low-grade rationality and be aware of the biases that impact our thinking. These include confirmation bias, conviction bias, appearance bias, group bias, blame bias, and superiority bias. To counter these biases, actively search for evidence that contradicts your ideas.[12]

The second step is to understand high-grade irrationality, which involves recognizing how our emotions influence our decision-making processes. By examining our emotions at their roots, we can gain a deeper understanding of our own reactions and increase our reaction time, allowing us to respond more thoughtfully in challenging situations.[13]

The third step focuses on strategies to bring out the rational side within us, a process that itself has six steps.

1. Knowing yourself thoroughly is crucial, and the first step in this process is to know yourself inwardly. By observing and understanding your own emotions, you can navigate through conflicts with a clearer mindset. Finding the balance between thinking and emotion is essential, as it enables you to make more rational decisions.[14]

2. Developing empathy is another crucial aspect of understanding human nature. Transforming self-love

into empathy is a powerful tool for building relationships and resolving conflicts. The empathic skill set consists of four components: the empathic attitude, which requires a flexible and open spirit; analytic empathy, which allows you to see through people's masks; observational skills, where constant observation helps you understand human behavior patterns; and the law of compulsive behavior, which teaches us that people rarely engage in behaviors just once.

3. Understanding human nature also means recognizing the law of covetousness. People desire what they cannot have, and by knowing when and how to withdraw, employing a touch of coldness and ambiguity, and creating rivalries of desire, you can become an object of desire and influence others.

4. Shortsightedness is another aspect of human nature that can hinder conflict resolution. To overcome this, we must detach ourselves from the heat of the moment and deepen our perspective. Engaging with individuals who can imagine larger impacts over time can help us overcome our own short-sighted thinking. Unintended consequences are often a result of shortsightedness, so being mindful of the potential effects of our actions down the line is crucial.

5. The law of defensiveness reminds us of how hard it is to resist someone who puts us in a good mood. By validating others' self-opinion and confirming their self-worth, we can create a positive atmosphere that promotes cooperation and resolves conflicts. Sharing both good and bad information about yourself and observing others' reactions can provide valuable insights into their character.

6. Last, we must recognize that each individual is unique in their DNA, brain wiring, and experiences. This uniqueness serves a purpose, and by discovering our calling and primal inclinations early in life, we can align ourselves with our true calling and achieve a higher sense of fulfillment.

Understanding the laws of human nature is the key to resolving conflict and creating unbreakable alliances. By becoming aware of our biases, understanding our emotions, and developing empathy, we can navigate conflicts more effectively. Additionally, recognizing the laws of covetousness, shortsightedness, and defensiveness allows us to approach conflicts with a calmer perspective. By embracing our uniqueness and discovering our purpose, we can achieve success and fulfillment in our personal and professional lives.

Deception Detection in Conflict Resolution

Deception detection is a skill set that many people find challenging in the behavioral world. Many people focus on such detection, but understand that if you are constantly looking for deception, you will find it—and this confirmation bias can cause you to miss out on other important aspects of communication.

I tend to approach behaviors that may indicate deception with curiosity rather than suspicion. When I notice incongruence between someone's words, body language, and tempo, I become curious about the underlying reasons for their behavior. I avoid getting too close to such people, to avoid creating a situation where I may be deceived. If I inadvertently find myself in a situation where someone has deceived me, I explore options for disengaging from the unhealthy relationship.

True deception is most commonly seen in executive dialogues from individuals who prioritize themselves above others and the mission. Once someone becomes comfortable with deception, all of their behavior and words become suspect. Stay clear of such individuals and maintain a healthy distance.

In his book *The Truth Detector*, my friend Jack Schafer introduces the concept of elicitation as a more effective approach to gaining true information. Elicitation is a truth detector that aims to uncover the truth before the opportunity for deception arises. This approach is based on the understanding that humans have been trying to detect lies for thousands of years without consistent and repeatable results.[15]

Creating the right environment for elicitation is crucial. People are more likely to talk to those they like and less likely to engage with those they don't like. Building rapport is thus the foundation of successful elicitation. When we lose our ego and focus on establishing rapport, we increase our chances of eliciting the veracity we desire.

Rapport acts as a bridge that connects two individuals in a positive manner. To build rapport, you must understand and utilize the big three nonverbal friend signals: the eyebrow flash, the head tilt, and the smile. Sincere smiles, in particular, release endorphins and create a positive atmosphere. It is important to differentiate between sincere and fake smiles, as people can easily pick up on insincerity.

Additionally, prolonged eye contact can indicate intense emotions, be they love or hostility. Following the golden rule of friendship, if we want people to like us, we must make them feel good about themselves. Our egos often hinder this process, but by using empathetic statements, we can keep the focus on the other person rather than ourselves.

Active listening is another crucial component of building rapport and eliciting information. It involves concentrating on what the other person is saying, waiting a moment before responding, showing nonverbal cues of interest, avoiding interruptions, and using empathetic statements to demonstrate one's attention.

When engaging in elicitation, leaving our egos at the door is essential, as it allows us to effectively use natural human behavior to our advantage. People have a natural desire to correct others, and by proactively eliciting information, we can provoke an ego-driven response. However, this technique requires us to overcome our own ego and intentionally lower our perceived social status, which can be challenging for our brains.

Furthermore, people have a natural need to talk about others, especially if it doesn't directly impact them. They also have a desire for recognition, which can lead them to reveal more information to prove their worthiness. People are naturally curious and have a void between what they know and what they want to know. They also struggle to keep secrets and often take pride in their professional accomplishments, making them more likely to share information freely.

To perform a basic elicitation, it is important to avoid asking direct questions, as they can alert the person and potentially produce a lie. Instead, be clear about the information you seek and create the right environment for elicitation. Use rapport-building techniques, such as the big three nonverbal friend signals (eyebrow flash, head tilt, smile), and start with small talk unrelated to the information you are seeking.[16]

There are many elicitation techniques, such as the presumptive statement, shouldering the truth, the third-party perspective, bracketing, curiosity, status manipulation, empathetic statements, and naïveté, and they are all fantastic at appealing to our laws of human nature. Each technique is designed to create the right conditions to encourage individuals to reveal the truth before they become aware of your intentions. But, since this book and section are focused on creating the allies we need in life, we will focus on allies as we continue our journey.[17]

Deception detection and elicitation are valuable tools in conflict resolution. By understanding natural human behavior and using various techniques, we can create an environment that encourages truth telling and helps us navigate through difficult conversations. These skills are essential for effective leadership and building unbreakable alliances.

The Dichotomy of Freedom and Discipline

In the intricate world of alliances, conflicts are inevitable. The challenge lies in evaluating and selecting the most suitable solution that resolves the conflict while maintaining the alliance's integrity. It requires a delicate balance between freedom and discipline—a dichotomy that holds the key to unbreakable alliances and lasting success.

The concept of freedom within alliances may seem paradoxical. After all, alliances are built on cooperation and shared goals. However, true freedom within an alliance stems from the ability to express thoughts and concerns openly, without fear of retribution. It is the freedom to engage in constructive dialogue, even when opinions differ, that fuels innovation and strengthens alliances.

Yet, the pursuit of freedom must be tempered with discipline. Discipline is not a form of punishment; it is a guiding force that sets boundaries and ensures the smooth functioning of the alliance. It demands consistency and a commitment to show up, even on the days when motivation wanes. Discipline empowers us to adhere to agreements and honor our commitments, fostering trust and reliability within the alliance.

In his book *Discipline Is Destiny*, Ryan Holiday discusses how the dichotomy of freedom and discipline extends beyond the realm of alliances. It is a path to personal growth and self-mastery. By embracing discipline and self-control, we elevate ourselves to a higher plane of existence. It is through discipline that we conquer our own limitations and achieve greatness.[18]

Greed, if left unchecked, can undermine even the strongest of alliances. It is the insatiable desire for more that moves the goalposts, blurring the lines between success and excess. However, the pleasure derived from excess is fleeting, leaving us perpetually unsatisfied. To achieve lasting success, we must find contentment and balance, resisting the allure of greed and focusing on the value we bring to the alliance.

Consistency is the superpower that distinguishes exceptional leaders. It is not about being superhuman every day; rather, it is about showing up consistently and putting in the work. The reward lies not only in the end result but also in the growth and self-discovery that occur along the journey. By enduring the challenges and staying committed, we conquer obstacles and achieve our goals.[19]

Fear of change and perfectionism are shackles that hinder progress. In a rapidly evolving world, adaptability is paramount. Leaders who embrace change and see it as an opportunity for growth are the ones who thrive in alliances. Similarly, the pursuit of perfection is a trap that stifles innovation and progress. Instead, we should embrace imperfections, learn from them, and continuously evolve.

As noted, discipline is not a punishment; it is a way of living. It is a conscious choice to act and behave in a manner that aligns with our goals and values. Self-control is not a life sentence; it is a liberating path to personal growth and success. By exercising discipline and self-control, we create the foundation for trust, reliability, and excellence within ourselves and our alliances.[20]

Rigidity is the antithesis of strength. When we cling rigidly to our beliefs and resist change, we become fragile and vulnerable. The ability to adapt and embrace new ideas is a hallmark of strong leadership and successful alliances. Flexibility allows us to navigate challenges with resilience, ensuring the longevity and effectiveness of our alliances.

To succeed in the realm of alliances, we must also be a good friend to ourselves. Taking care of our physical and mental well-being, setting healthy boundaries, and practicing self-compassion are crucial aspects of leadership. By prioritizing self-care, we show up as our best selves, capable of cultivating meaningful connections and inspiring others within our alliances.

Ultimately, the power to create unbreakable alliances and achieve lasting success lies within our choices. We have the authority to choose our actions, attitudes, and responses to challenges. By embracing the dichotomy of freedom and discipline, we unlock the path to success, empowering ourselves and our alliances to reach new heights.

Ten Actions

1. Prioritize maintaining relationships and trust over immediate material outcomes in conflicts. Compromise and let go of certain outcomes if necessary.

2. Make an effort to understand others' context and perspective during conflicts. Engage in thoughtful conversations and ask open-ended questions.

3. Take ownership of your own behavior and actions in conflicts. Reflect on how your actions may have made the other person feel unsafe and adjust your approach accordingly.

4. Engage in active listening and empathetic communication to understand the other person's viewpoint. Find common ground and prioritize the relationship over immediate outcomes.

5. Practice curiosity and nonjudgment when encountering conflicting ideas. Take the time to explore the context behind those ideas and seek to understand the reasons behind them.

6. Listen actively to your ally's needs and concerns when conflicts arise. Apologize if necessary and seek their thoughts and opinions. Validate their feelings and work toward finding common ground.

7. Simplify your approach to conflicts by focusing on effective communication. Ask open-ended questions to understand your ally's needs and concerns. Look for areas of compromise and validate their thoughts and opinions.

8. Cultivate humility and self-awareness to counter ego-driven actions. Seek feedback and be open to constructive criticism from others. Embrace continuous learning and growth.

9. Prioritize effective conflict resolution over ego-driven desires. Approach conflicts with a clear and open mind, actively listening to the perspectives of others. Seek common ground and resolutions that benefit all parties involved.

10. Develop self-leadership for strength and composure during conflicts. Engage in self-reflection and personal development activities. Practice mindfulness and curiosity to approach conflicts with clarity, and focus on finding mutually beneficial solutions.

6

CONTEXT

The Recipe for Acceptance and Understanding

How wonderful it is that nobody need wait a single moment before starting to improve the world.
—Anne Frank

Building Stronger Connections Through Understanding

In the early stages of my career, I was tasked with leading a team of diverse individuals from different backgrounds and experiences. One particular team member, let's call him Dylan, always seemed to have ideas that were completely different from mine. I found myself dismissing his ideas without much consideration, thinking that my own were superior.

One day, as I was reflecting on my leadership approach, I came across a quote by Neil deGrasse Tyson that struck a chord within me: "One of the greatest pains to human nature is the pain of a new idea." Those words made me realize that I had been shutting down Dylan's ideas simply because they were unfamiliar to me.

Determined to change my approach, I decided to take the time to understand Dylan's context. I invited him for a coffee outside of the office, and as we sat down, I asked him about his background, his experiences, and what motivated him in his work. What I discovered was truly eye opening.

Dylan grew up in a completely different environment than I did, faced challenges that I couldn't even fathom, and had a unique perspective that came from his diverse background. As I listened to him share his thoughts and ideas, I realized the immense value they held. His ideas were not inferior; they were just different, and it was through understanding his context that I could truly appreciate their worth.

From that moment on, I made it a point to approach every team member with the understanding that they had put in time and effort to come up with their ideas. I recognized that their perspectives were shaped by their own unique contexts, just as mine were. By embracing this understanding, I was able to create a team environment where everyone felt valued, respected, and heard.

That experience with Dylan taught me the power of context in building alliances. By taking the time to understand someone's background and experiences, we can create stronger connections and tap into a wealth of ideas and perspectives that we might have otherwise overlooked. It was a turning point in my leadership journey, and one that has continued to shape my approach to building unbreakable alliances ever since.

In today's world, diversity and inclusion are hot topics that often divide us. But what if I told you that understanding context is the key to bridging those gaps and building unbreakable alliances? In my years of experience in leadership and human behavior, I have come to understand that context is the bedrock for success in any endeavor, especially when it comes to creating strong alliances.

So, what exactly is context? It's the ability to step outside of ourselves and see the world through someone else's eyes. It's about understanding their background, experiences, beliefs, and social and economic status. When we take the time to truly dive deep and understand the decision-making process of others, we can begin to build bridges of collaboration and partnership.

Understanding someone's context means understanding their thought processes, motivations, agenda, strengths, and personal challenges. It also means understanding their biases. Biases are not inherently good or bad; they simply exist. And by understanding someone's biases, we can better navigate the complexities of building alliances.

But context is not just about understanding the other person; it's also about approaching every individual with respect and acknowledging the time and effort they have put into their own thoughts and opinions. Imagine if someone dismissed your ideas without giving them fair consideration; it would be insulting and likely would trigger your insecurities and defenses. The same goes for doing so to others. By recognizing the effort people put into their decisions and viewpoints, we can create a foundation of mutual respect and understanding.

In his book *Starry Messenger*, Neil deGrasse Tyson speaks of the cosmic perspective, which is closely tied to the concept of context. It is the idea of looking at the world from a broader lens, seeing our place in the vastness of the universe. This cosmic perspective can be a wake-up call to civilization, reminding us of the interconnectedness of all things and the importance of collaboration and unity.[1]

When we embrace a cosmic perspective, we realize that opinions are just that—opinions. What truly matters is the search for data, for knowledge, for a deeper understanding of the behavior of nature. As Leonardo da Vinci once said, "The noblest pleasure is the joy of understanding." It is this joy that should drive us in our quest for alliances.[2]

A cosmic perspective also helps us disconnect from our egos and engage in accountability. We start to see ourselves as part of something much bigger, and this perspective enables us to resolve conflicts with empathy and understanding. We recognize that baselines, or common ground, can be found when we view things from a cosmic perspective.

Understanding context is crucial for building strong alliances. It allows us to see the world through someone else's eyes, to understand their motivations, biases, and decision-making processes. By embracing a cosmic perspective, we can bridge divides, find common ground, and work toward a better future together. So, let us strive to approach every interaction with an open mind and a willingness to understand, for it is through context that we can create unbreakable allies.

The Power of Now:
Building Unbreakable Alliances

In the quest to build unbreakable alliances, there is one practical technique that stands above the rest: curiosity. Through curiosity, we can truly dive deep into understanding others, leveraging context, and building trust and rapport. In this section, we will explore the transformative power of curiosity, drawing inspiration from Eckhart Tolle's *The Power of Now*.[3]

Curiosity is the key to understanding others and their motivations. To begin, we must be aware of our own biases and let go of our personal agendas. By being present in the now, as Tolle suggests, we can silence the noise in our minds and truly see others for who they are. Approaching each interaction with the curiosity and wonder of a child, we open ourselves up to experiencing the world through their eyes.[4]

To build trust and rapport, we must uncover the origin story of our allies. This involves understanding the factors that have shaped them, both genetically and through their life experiences. By delving into their origin story, we gain insights into their motivations and purpose in life. This knowledge allows us to connect with them more deeply and build stronger alliances.

Leadership is about being a catalyst for change and giving courage to others. By approaching every interaction with curiosity, we create an environment where others feel seen and heard. This empowers them to embrace inner change and live their purpose. As leaders, our role is not to give others what we have, but to help them find what they already possess within themselves. This requires us to choose our words carefully, serving others rather than ourselves.

In our pursuit of building unbreakable alliances, we must recognize the internal tormentor that resides within others. Negative emotions and behaviors often attract the same in others. By being present in the now and offering genuine curiosity and understanding, we can help others navigate their inner turmoil and find peace.

Accepting the present moment and acting in alignment with it is a crucial lesson for leaders. It requires us to work with the now, making it our ally rather than our enemy. By being the observer and silent watcher of our thoughts and reactions, we can cope with the present moment and make effective decisions.

True power lies within, not in exerting power over others. As leaders, we must let go of our ego-driven identities, beliefs, and opinions. By embracing vulnerability and being present in the now, we can build unbreakable alliances. This means recognizing that our true identities are not defined by external factors but by our inner essence.

Imagine you are a leader tasked with forming a strategic alliance with a potential partner for your business. You know that building trust and rapport is crucial for the success of this alliance. To do so, you decide to employ the power of curiosity.

You begin by setting aside your own agenda and biases, as Eckhart Tolle suggests in *The Power of Now*. You enter the meeting genuinely curious about the other party's motivations and purpose in life. Instead of jumping straight into business matters, you take the time to ask open-ended questions and actively listen to their responses.

As the conversation progresses, you notice an opportunity to delve deeper into their origin story. You inquire about their background, upbringing, and the experiences that have shaped them. By doing so, you gain valuable insights into their values, aspirations, and the driving forces behind their decisions.

Being fully present in the now, you let go of any preconceived notions or judgments that may arise. You approach the interaction with the curiosity and wonder of a child, eager to learn and understand. This fosters a sense of trust and connection, allowing the other party to feel seen and heard.

As a leader, you recognize that your role is not to impose your ideas or solutions upon the other party. Instead, you focus on helping them uncover their own strengths and resources. By choosing your words carefully and serving their needs, you empower them to find the answers they seek within themselves.

Throughout the conversation, you remain aware of any internal tormentors that may be affecting the other party. Negative emotions or past experiences might hinder their ability to fully engage in the alliance. With genuine curiosity and understanding, you create a safe space for them to address these issues, offering support and guidance along the way.

By accepting and embracing the present moment, you work with the now rather than against it. You understand that true power lies within, not in exerting power over others. As the leader, you lead by example, embracing vulnerability and encouraging others to do the same. This vulnerability strengthens the bond between you and your potential ally, laying the foundation for an unbreakable alliance.

In this example, curiosity becomes the driving force behind building trust and rapport. By being present in the now and genuinely interested in the other party, you create a space for open dialogue, understanding, and connection. Through curiosity, you set the stage for a successful and unbreakable alliance, based on mutual respect and shared goals.

Embracing Differences: The Power of Unlikely Partnerships

Jesse was reserved, analytical, and detail oriented. While I was the one who would come up with big ideas and initiate operations, he was the one who would ensure that every step was carefully planned and executed. Our partnership was a perfect example of how working with individuals who are different from oneself can present both challenges and opportunities.

At first, our differences did present some challenges. Our approaches to problem solving and decision making often varied. I would want to jump right into action, while Jesse would want to analyze every possible outcome before making a move. This led to some disagreements and heated debates.

However, these challenges also presented opportunities for growth and learning. Through our discussions and debates, we were able to understand each other's perspectives more deeply. We learned to appreciate the value that each of us brought to the table and how our strengths complemented each other.

For example, one case tasked us with infiltrating a highly secretive intelligence organization. I had come up with a bold plan to gain their trust and gather crucial information. Jesse, on the other hand, had reservations about the risks involved and insisted on conducting a thorough analysis before proceeding.

Instead of butting heads and insisting on our own ways, we decided to listen to each other and find a middle ground. We combined my bold plan with Jesse's meticulous analysis, ensuring that we had a solid strategy in place while also taking calculated risks. This allowed us to successfully infiltrate the organization and gather the necessary intelligence to change the course of our national security policy.

Throughout our partnership, we learned to leverage our differences to our advantage. While I brought the energy and enthusiasm to build relationships and forge alliances, Jesse brought the attention to detail and careful planning that prevented us from making costly mistakes. Together, we were able to achieve more than we could have individually.

The key takeaway: Embracing diversity in partnerships can lead to greater success. When we surround ourselves with individuals who think differently from us, we open ourselves up to new perspectives and ideas. We challenge our own biases and expand our horizons. By leveraging each other's strengths and compensating for each other's weaknesses, we create a powerful, unbreakable alliance.

So, when faced with the opportunity to work with individuals who are different from you, embrace the challenges and seize the opportunities for growth and learning. By doing so, you will become a better leader while creating unbreakable allies who will help you succeed.

Overcoming Communication Barriers and Fostering Understanding in Diverse Alliances

For leaders to navigate the complexities of diverse alliances and overcome communication barriers, they must employ specific strategies and approaches. The first and foremost requirement for effective leadership is humility, as highlighted in *The Dichotomy of Leadership* by Jocko Willink and Leif Babin. Humility allows leaders to approach communication with an open mind and a willingness to listen and understand.[5]

To foster understanding within diverse alliances, leaders need to practice silence and patience. Taking the time to truly listen and seek clarity will enable leaders to grasp others' perspectives and viewpoints. Additionally, simplicity should be a guiding principle when communicating with alliances of diverse people. Complex language or jargon can hinder understanding, so leaders should strive to convey their message in a clear, straightforward manner.

One valuable resource for enhancing communication within diverse alliances is the four keys of communication, as outlined earlier. These keys focus on shifting the attention from oneself to the other person, seeking their thoughts and opinions, and discovering their priorities, challenges, and pain points. Validating others without judgment and empowering them with choices are also crucial aspects of effective communication.

Be sure to strike a balance when employing these strategies, however. The goal is to work toward fostering understanding without compromising the mission or the team. Leaders must remember that their ultimate responsibility is to the success of the alliance as a whole. This requires finding the delicate balance between building strong relationships and fulfilling the objectives of the alliance.

The Dichotomy of Leadership also emphasizes the need for leaders to own their responsibilities while empowering others. Extreme ownership can lead to micromanaging, stifling innovation and growth within the team; yet, being too hands-off can result in a lack of vision and coordination. Leaders must strive to find the right balance between ownership and decentralized command, allowing their team members the freedom to excel while providing guidance and support when needed.[6]

Another crucial aspect of fostering understanding within diverse alliances is the ability to hold people accountable without holding their hands. Leaders should explain the reasons behind their actions, allow individuals to self-regulate, and spot-inspect their progress. By highlighting the impact of their actions on the alliance as a whole, leaders can effectively promote accountability and cultivate a sense of ownership among team members.[7]

Leadership also involves a continuous process of learning and growth. Hard training, as emphasized in *The Dichotomy of Leadership*, is essential to building capable leaders at every level. Leaders must be willing to train hard and train smart, focusing on fundamentals, realism, and repetition. Debriefing is an integral part of the training process, providing an opportunity for reflection and improvement.[8]

Leaders can overcome communication barriers and foster understanding within diverse alliances by practicing humility, silence, and patience. They need to strike the right balance between ownership and decentralized command, accountability and empowerment, and planning and adaptability. By embracing these principles, leaders can navigate the complexities of diverse alliances and guide their teams toward success.

The Power of Curiosity in Building Strong Alliances

In the bustling metropolis of Cityville, there was a renowned business leader named Hannah. Known for her ability to form unbreakable alliances, she was hailed as a master of collaboration. People marveled at her knack for bringing together diverse individuals and creating successful partnerships.

One fateful day, as Hannah was perusing a local bookstore, a book caught her attention: *Cracking the Curiosity Code*, by Diane Hamilton. Intrigued by the title, she couldn't resist picking it up and scanning its pages.[9]

Within the book, Hannah discovered a treasure trove of insights on the power of curiosity in alliance building. She learned that curiosity goes beyond being a mere trait; it can transform ordinary collaborations into extraordinary partnerships.

Eager to put this newfound knowledge into action, Hannah decided to test the power of curiosity in her own leadership journey. She began by organizing a unique networking event, inviting professionals from diverse industries. Rather than engaging in superficial small talk, Hannah encouraged attendees to have deep conversations by asking thought-provoking questions.

As the event unfolded, something magical happened. The room buzzed with energy as people shared their stories, experiences, and aspirations. Genuine connections were formed, and a sense of trust and camaraderie permeated the atmosphere.

Inspired by the success of the event, Hannah continued to embrace curiosity in her daily interactions. She made a conscious effort to ask open-ended questions, to truly listen and understand others' perspectives. Whether it was during team meetings or client presentations, curiosity became her secret weapon in building strong alliances.

One particular alliance stood out among the rest. Hannah had always admired a fellow entrepreneur named Michael, known for his innovative ideas and unwavering determination. Determined to form an alliance with him, Hannah approached him with genuine curiosity, eager to understand his perspective and learn from his expertise.

To her delight, Michael enthusiastically reciprocated her curiosity. He was impressed by Hannah's genuine interest and willingness to listen without judgment. The two entrepreneurs soon found themselves collaborating on a groundbreaking project that would reshape their industry. Their alliance became unbreakable, built on a foundation of trust, mutual respect, and a shared curiosity to explore new possibilities.

Word of Hannah's remarkable ability to form unbreakable alliances spread like wildfire. Other leaders sought her guidance in building their own successful collaborations. Hannah became known as the "Curiosity Catalyst," a visionary leader who harnessed the power of curiosity to bring people together and create extraordinary alliances.

Hannah's story serves as a reminder to all aspiring leaders that curiosity is not just a trait, but a superpower. By embracing curiosity, we can unlock the potential within ourselves and others, creating unbreakable alliances that lead to remarkable success in the ever-evolving business landscape.

Curiosity is a trait that is often associated with successful leaders. In the context of alliance building, curiosity plays a vital role in fostering strong relationships and creating unbreakable allies. But what exactly does curiosity mean in this context, and what are its benefits? Let's explore these questions using insights from Diane Hamilton's book *Cracking the Curiosity Code*.[10]

Curiosity, in the context of alliance building, can be defined as a deep interest in understanding and getting to know others without judgment. It is about being present for the people in your personal and professional lives, and genuinely looking forward to collaborating with them. Think about the individuals who light up your life: the friends, family members, colleagues, or leaders who you eagerly anticipate spending time with. Chances are, these individuals exhibit a core behavior of curiosity toward you. They show a genuine interest in who you are, without judging you, and this creates a strong bond of trust and collaboration.

The benefits of curiosity in alliance building are numerous. When you approach others with curiosity, you demonstrate that you value and trust them. This builds a sense of psychological safety and encourages open communication. Curiosity fuels motivation by providing the "why" behind the goals and objectives of an alliance. It ignites excitement and drives engagement, making the alliance members more invested in achieving success together.

Leaders who inspire curiosity in others are often the greatest leaders. They create an environment where questions are encouraged and curiosity is rewarded. They understand that answers alone do not solve problems; rather, the questions lead to innovative solutions. These leaders embrace the unknown and have the courage to say, "I don't know." They constantly seek out criticism and feedback, recognizing the value it brings in driving improvement.

However, it is important to note that fear can hinder curiosity. People may worry that curiosity will expose their lack of knowledge or make them feel vulnerable. But the opposite of fear is not bravery;

it is curiosity. Embracing curiosity allows us to overcome fear and expand our knowledge and understanding.[11]

To harness the power of curiosity in alliance building, consider three key actions:

1. Ask questions and show a genuine interest in others. This demonstrates that you value their perspectives and experiences.
2. Trust the individuals in your alliance and create an environment where they feel safe to share their thoughts and ideas.
3. Track the progress and outcomes of your alliance, using curiosity as a driving force for continuous improvement and growth.

Curiosity is a powerful tool for building strong alliances. By embracing curiosity, leaders can encourage trust, collaboration, and engagement within their alliances. It is through curiosity that innovative solutions are discovered, and unbreakable allies are created. So, let us embrace curiosity and make it a cornerstone of our leadership journey.

Opening the Door to Innovation: The Power of "What If?" Questions and Embracing Failure

Let's explore two powerful techniques that leaders can adopt to foster curiosity within their alliance relationships: asking "What if?" questions and embracing failure as a learning opportunity.

"What if?" questions have the incredible ability to open up a world of possibilities. When leaders encourage their team members to think creatively and explore different scenarios, they create an environment where curiosity can thrive. By posing questions like, "What if we took a completely different approach?" or "What if we had unlimited resources?," leaders challenge their teams to break free from conventional thinking and consider new perspectives.

Let's consider a real-life example to illustrate the impact of "What if?" questions on alliance development. A company facing a seemingly insurmountable challenge recognized the need for fresh ideas and perspectives. During a brainstorming session, the leaders posed a series of "What if?" questions, inviting their team members to think outside the box. This simple technique sparked curiosity and ignited a wave of innovative thinking. Ultimately, it led to a breakthrough idea that solved the company's problem and strengthened their alliance relationships.

But fostering curiosity doesn't stop at asking questions. It also involves creating a safe space for failure. Leaders must understand that innovation often requires taking risks, and not all attempts will yield immediate success. Embracing failure means making it a part of the budget and plan, acknowledging that things may go sideways.

By investing in failure, leaders communicate a powerful message to their teams: it's okay to take chances and make mistakes. Failure is not something to be feared or punished but rather an opportunity for growth and learning. This mindset shift creates an environment where team members feel safe to experiment, innovate, and contribute their unique perspectives to the alliance.

To ensure that the lessons from failure are not lost, leaders should implement after-action reviews. These provide a structured process for analyzing what went wrong, what could have been done differently, and how to improve in the future. By creating a safe place to learn from failure, leaders promote a culture of continuous improvement and growth within their alliance relationships.

The power of "What if?" questions and embracing failure as a learning opportunity cannot be understated. These techniques not only foster curiosity within alliance relationships but also pave the way for innovation and success. By encouraging teams to think outside the box and creating a safe space for taking risks, leaders can unlock the full potential of their alliances and create unbreakable bonds. Let's therefore embrace curiosity, ask "What if?" questions, and view failure as a stepping stone toward growth and achievement.

Creating Psychological Safety for Open Dialogue and Collaboration

In today's business landscape, success no longer depends solely on individual achievements. The ability to form strong alliances and collaborate effectively has become crucial for achieving lasting success. However, creating a safe place and a welcome environment within these alliances is essential for nurturing open dialogue and collaboration. Let's explore how leaders can create psychological safety, where allies feel comfortable sharing their ideas and opinions.

In Simon Sinek's book *Start with Why*, he emphasizes the importance of purpose and belonging in inspiring others. Leaders who focus on manipulation rather than inspiration may achieve short-term gains, but they fail to win loyalty and long-term commitment. Manipulation leads to transactions, not loyalty. To create psychological safety, leaders must start with the purpose, cause, or belief that drives their organization. People don't buy what you do; they buy why you do it. When leaders can articulate and share the why behind their actions, they inspire others to take action as well.[12]

Trust plays a crucial role in establishing psychological safety. Trust comes from a feeling of belonging and is built through clarity, discipline, and consistency. Leaders who cultivate trust create an environment where good ideas can flourish. They find good fits within their organization, hiring for attitude rather than just skills. Ernest Shackleton's advertisement for his Antarctic expedition serves as a great example of this principle. He didn't seek individuals seeking power or personal benefits; instead, he sought those who were committed to a greater mission and purpose.[13]

Leaders who lead with purpose and serve those who serve them gain trust and loyalty. They don't set out to impress everyone but rather focus on creating an environment where great ideas can happen. These leaders understand that communication isn't just about speaking; it's about listening. They speak less and listen more, seeking to understand the needs and perspectives of others. By doing so, they overcome obstacles and skepticism, building trust and nurturing collaboration.

In his book *Leaders Eat Last*, Sinek reveals the deep benefits of creating trust within organizations. Leaders who prioritize the needs of others above their own inspire their teams to dream more, learn more, and do more. Sinek introduces the concept of a "circle of safety," where individuals feel a sense of belonging and shared values. When this circle of safety is strong, trust, cooperation, and problem solving thrive. It allows individuals to face external dangers with confidence, as they trust that their fellow allies will protect and support them.[14]

To create a circle of safety, leaders must focus on building trust and developing empathy. Trust is earned by extending trust to others, and empathy is the single greatest asset a leader possesses. When individuals feel valued and cared for at work, their stress levels decrease and engagement increases. Gallup polls have shown that when bosses ignore or criticize employees, they disengage. However, when bosses acknowledge and appreciate the strengths of their employees, engagement soars.

Leaders must also understand the chemical reactions that occur within the human body. Four chemicals—endorphins, dopamine, serotonin, and oxytocin—play a significant role in our behavior and emotions. Endorphins and dopamine drive us to achieve goals and experience pleasure. Serotonin and oxytocin, on the other hand, foster trust, belonging, and empathy. By understanding and harnessing these chemicals, leaders can create an environment where individuals feel valued, motivated, and connected.

Leaders who prioritize people and build a culture of trust can unleash innovation and collaboration within their alliances. Trust allows individuals to share successes and failures, leading to collective problem solving and growth. Leaders must remember that their actions and behaviors set the tone for their organization's culture. By walking the halls, listening, and connecting with their teams, leaders can nurture a culture of trust, cooperation, and stability.

Creating psychological safety within alliances is crucial for developing open dialogue and collaboration. Leaders must focus on belonging, purpose, and trust to inspire and motivate their allies. By prioritizing the needs of others, listening, and encouraging empathy, leaders can build a circle of safety where individuals feel valued and connected. This, in turn, leads to increased engagement, innovation, and enduring success.

Promoting Constructive Feedback and Respectful Disagreement Within Alliances

To foster a culture of open communication and diverse perspectives within alliances, leaders must employ strategies that promote constructive feedback and respectful disagreement. By doing so, leaders can ensure that every voice is valued and heard, ultimately leading to stronger and more effective alliances.

One key strategy is to use the four keys to communication mentioned throughout the book: seeking others' thoughts and opinions, talking in terms of priorities, validating them through nonjudgmental curiosity, and empowering others with choices. This approach encourages individuals to share their perspectives and ideas, while also feeling acknowledged and empowered. By actively seeking input from alliance members, leaders can access the wealth of knowledge and expertise that exist within the group, leading to more well-rounded and informed decision making.

Another effective technique for promoting constructive feedback and respectful disagreement is to implement the principles outlined in Reed Hastings and Erin Meyer's book, *No Rules Rules: Netflix and the Culture of Reinvention*. This groundbreaking book highlights the importance of valuing people over process, fostering innovation over efficiency, and implementing very few controls. By leading with context instead of control, leaders can create an environment that encourages open dialogue and diverse perspectives.[15]

One key aspect of inviting constructive feedback and respectful disagreement is that it creates a safe environment for individuals to express their thoughts and ideas without fear of judgment or rejection. Netflix's culture, outlined in *No Rules Rules*—demonstrates the power of honesty, nimble flexibility, and talent density in creating such an environment. By providing a generous severance package for inadequate performers and cultivating a culture of candor, leaders can ensure that alliance members feel secure in sharing their opinions and ideas.[16]

To promote constructive feedback and respectful disagreement within alliances, leaders must also model these behaviors and be transparent in their actions and decision making. Trust is a crucial component of effective communication. Leaders can build trust by always acting in the best interests of the company, being a resource for their people, and avoiding actions that hinder others' goals. By giving employees freedom and responsibility, leaders can demonstrate trust and empower individuals to take ownership of their work.

Transparency is another key element in promoting constructive feedback and respectful disagreement within alliances. Keeping secrets or spinning the truth can erode trust and hinder open communication. Leaders should strive to share information that is relevant to employees' situational awareness, providing them with the necessary context to make informed decisions and take ownership of their work. By sharing wins and mistakes openly, leaders create a culture of transparency and encourage open dialogue.

Innovation and feedback go hand in hand, and leaders should create a culture that fosters dissent and encourages sharing ideas.

By embracing a feedback loop and maximizing candor, leaders can develop an environment where constructive feedback and respectful disagreement are both valued and celebrated. Leaders must discourage gossip and emphasize the importance of providing feedback with positive intent, focusing on offering insights rather than being a jerk.

The leaders of two technology companies in a high-stakes alliance understood the importance of promoting constructive feedback and respectful disagreement for driving innovation and success. They implemented various techniques to ensure that diverse perspectives were valued and heard within the alliance.

During a critical strategy meeting, the leaders initiated a discussion on a new product-development approach. They sought thoughts and opinions from all alliance members, emphasizing the importance of each individual's unique perspective. One of the engineers, Lena, expressed her concerns about the feasibility of the proposed approach, highlighting potential technical challenges that could arise. Rather than dismissing her opinion, the leaders listened attentively, validating her expertise and acknowledging the value of her input.

To further encourage constructive feedback, the leaders framed the discussion in terms of priorities. They highlighted the shared goal of delivering an innovative product to the market and explained how the proposed approach aligned with that objective. This helped Lena and other alliance members understand the bigger picture and view their differing perspectives as valuable contributions to achieving the common goal.

Recognizing the importance of offering choices, the leaders presented alternative approaches and asked alliance members to provide their preferences. They encouraged open dialogue, inviting everyone to share their concerns, ideas, and potential solutions. Through this process, they created a collaborative environment where alliance members felt empowered to take ownership of their ideas and contribute to the decision-making process.

The leaders also emphasized the principles outlined in *No Rules Rules*. They created a safe and inclusive environment where everyone felt comfortable expressing their opinions. They reinforced the importance of providing feedback with positive intent, focusing on insights rather than personal attacks, and discouraging any form of gossip or backstabbing.

In the end, the alliance members engaged in a spirited yet respectful discussion. Through constructive feedback and courteous disagreement, they collectively arrived at a modified approach that addressed Lena's concerns while still aligning with the overall objectives. The result was a stronger, more innovative product development strategy that integrated diverse perspectives and expertise.

This anecdote highlights how the techniques of seeking thoughts and opinions, talking in terms of priorities, validating contributions, and offering choices can create a culture of constructive feedback and respectful disagreement within alliances. By implementing these techniques, leaders can harness the collective intelligence of the alliance members, driving innovation and achieving success together.

Promoting constructive feedback and respectful disagreement within alliances requires leaders to employ various strategies and techniques. By seeking thoughts and opinions, leading with context, fostering a culture of candor, and embracing transparency, leaders can create an environment where diverse perspectives are valued and heard. Through these practices, alliances can thrive and achieve success.

Embracing the Path to Unbreakable Alliances

As we conclude this chapter, I want to leave you with some final thoughts and advice on how to create unbreakable alliances. Throughout our journey, we have explored the importance of context, curiosity, and creating a safe environment. Let's bring these all together and embrace these principles wholeheartedly.

First and foremost, never underestimate the power of context. Immerse yourself in biographies and history; if reading is not your preferred mode, turn to audiobooks or other media that suit your style. By consuming information related to your own interests and those of your alliance members, you gain a deeper understanding of their perspectives. This understanding allows you to communicate more effectively and strengthen connections. Remember, context is the foundation upon which successful alliances are built.

Curiosity is the fuel that drives alliance building. Approach others with genuine interest and a desire to learn from them. Ask questions, actively listen, and seek to understand their motivations, aspirations, and values. By embracing curiosity, we create an environment that encourages open dialogue, collaboration, and the free exchange of ideas. Curiosity is the catalyst for unlocking the full potential of our alliances.

Creating a safe environment is also vital for building unbreakable alliances. Actively listen to others, demonstrate respect, and empathize with their perspectives. Make sure everyone feels heard, valued, and included. When people feel safe and accepted, they are more willing to share their ideas, challenge conventional thinking, and take risks. It is within this safe space that true innovation and growth can thrive.

In our journey toward creating unbreakable alliances, remember that building strong connections takes time and effort. We need to continuously learn, adapt, and grow. By applying the principles of context, curiosity, and creating a safe environment, you will forge unbreakable alliances that withstand the test of time. Embrace the challenges and setbacks as opportunities for growth. View each interaction as a chance to strengthen your alliance-building skills and deepen your understanding of others.

These alliances will serve as the bedrock for your success, both personally and professionally. Embrace the path to unbreakable alliances and watch as your relationships flourish and your goals become reality.

Remember, the journey toward success is not a solitary one. Together, we can navigate the complex landscape of alliance building and pave the way for a future filled with lasting connections and achievements.

Ten Actions

1. Invest time in actively listening and engaging in conversations with others, seeking to understand their unique perspectives and experiences.
2. Practice empathy and respect when engaging with others. Give their ideas fair consideration, even if they differ from your own.
3. Cultivate a cosmic perspective by seeking knowledge, understanding nature's behavior, and embracing a mindset of exploration and discovery.

4. Reach out to a colleague or professional contact who has a different skill set or expertise than your own. Propose a collaborative project or partnership that leverages each other's strengths.

5. Schedule a meeting with your team or colleagues to discuss a challenging problem or project. Encourage everyone to share their ideas and perspectives, creating an inclusive environment where all voices are heard.

6. Reflect on past partnerships or collaborations where differences led to success. Identify specific instances where your partner's strengths complemented your own. Use these insights to seek out similar partnerships in the future and leverage the power of diverse perspectives.

7. Seek out different perspectives and opinions, even if they contradict your own. Schedule a meeting or discussion with individuals from diverse backgrounds and actively listen to their perspectives and opinions.

8. Review and simplify your message before sending any important communication. Cut unnecessary jargon or complex language that may hinder understanding.

9. Identify a specific task or project that can be delegated to a team member. Clearly communicate the objective, provide necessary resources, and empower them to make decisions and take ownership of the task.

10. Encourage team members to think outside the box by regularly posing "What if?" questions during brainstorming sessions or team meetings. Challenge them to explore different scenarios and consider unconventional approaches to problems.

7

BUILD

The Power of Long-Term Alliances:
A Tale of Collaboration and Triumph

*You have power over your mind—not outside
events. Realize this, and you will find strength.*
—Marcus Aurelius

Let me take you back to a time when I found myself in a high-stakes mission that required the power of long-term alliances to succeed. It was a collaboration between the CIA, the British, and myself that showcased the true potential and strength of these unbreakable relationships.

Our objective was to recruit a high-level foreign intelligence officer we'll refer to as Agent X, known for his exceptional skills and invaluable access to sensitive information. Agent X held the key to unraveling the inner workings of a dangerous enemy organization. However, convincing him to switch sides was no easy task.

I knew that to succeed, I needed to leverage the combined expertise and resources of the CIA and the British. Our greatest assets in this operation were our long-standing alliances, built on trust and collaboration.

Together, we launched a meticulous planning process, analyzing Agent X's background, motivations, and what some call "vulnerabilities" (I refer to them as "pain points"). Drawing upon our collective knowledge and expertise, we crafted a strategy that would appeal to his desires for a better future and the opportunity to make a difference.

Through our long-term alliances, we were able to pool resources, intelligence, and operational capabilities. The CIA's extensive network of informants provided crucial insights, while the expertise of the British in covert operations ensured utmost discretion and effectiveness. We formed an unbreakable force.

Months of careful planning and coordination brought us to the crucial moment of meeting with Agent X. In a secure location, I stood alongside my CIA and British counterparts, presenting a compelling case that showcased the advantages of joining our side. The trust we had built over years of collaboration and shared successes resonated with Agent X, who saw the potential for a brighter future and a chance to make a real impact.

Through the power of our long-term alliances, we successfully recruited Agent X, transforming him into a valuable asset for our respective intelligence agencies. His information proved invaluable to disrupting numerous high-level operations and protecting countless lives.

This story testifies to the immense power of long-term alliances. By leveraging the strengths, resources, and expertise of each partner, we achieved a remarkable outcome. Our shared commitment to collaboration, trust, and a common goal resulted in a triumphant success that would have been unimaginable without our unbreakable alliances.

This story also serves as a reminder of the potential that lies within long-term alliances: by building strong and enduring relationships, organizations can overcome seemingly insurmountable challenges and achieve extraordinary results.

Fast-Forward to Now

In the fast-paced and ever-changing business world, building and maintaining strong alliances is crucial for lasting success. These alliances not only provide stability and reliability but also offer a multitude of benefits that can propel organizations to new heights. Let's explore the power of building long-term alliances and uncover the key advantages that come with investing time and effort into establishing unbreakable allies.

Stability and Reliability: One of the most significant benefits of long-term alliances is the stability and reliability they bring to business relationships. Trust and understanding develop over time, creating a strong foundation for collaboration. As a result, operations run smoother, and uncertainty is significantly reduced. Long-term alliances bring peace of mind because you have dependable partners by your side.

Shared Resources and Expertise: Long-term alliances often involve pooling resources, knowledge, and expertise. This sharing can enhance capabilities and bring a competitive advantage. By leveraging each other's strengths, partners can achieve common goals and tackle complex challenges more effectively. Joint investments in research and development, manufacturing facilities, or marketing campaigns can be more cost effective than individual efforts. Through alliances, you can tap into a wealth of resources that otherwise might have been inaccessible.

Market Expansion: Another major advantage of long-term alliances is their ability to facilitate market expansion. By leveraging each partner's distribution networks, customer base, or geographic reach, alliances open up new markets and customers that may have been challenging to enter independently. This expansion can be a game changer, allowing organizations to reach a broader audience and increase their market share.

Risk Mitigation: In a constantly shifting business landscape, uncertainties and unforeseen challenges are inevitable. However, by sharing risks through long-term alliances, organizations can better withstand these challenges and adapt more effectively. Your allies offer a support system that can help navigate through tough times and mitigate potential risks. This shared resilience is a powerful asset that can provide a competitive boost.

Learning and Innovation: Long-term alliances provide a fertile ground for learning and innovation. By exchanging ideas, best practices, and knowledge, partners can learn from each other's experiences, technologies, and approaches. This continuous learning and innovation lead to improved problem solving and the development of cutting-edge solutions. As the saying goes, "Two heads are better than one"; in the realm of long-term alliances, this rings especially true.

Brand Enhancement and Reputation: Collaborating with reputable and established partners through long-term alliances can enhance a company's brand image and credibility. By associating with trusted and respected allies, organizations can increase customer trust, improve market perception, and elevate their brand value. This enhanced reputation can open doors to new opportunities and lead stakeholders to perceive the firm more positively.

By combining complementary strengths and resources, organizations can differentiate themselves in the market and gain a competitive edge. Long-term alliances provide a solid foundation for success, fostering stability, shared resources, market expansion, risk mitigation, learning, innovation, and brand enhancement. Investing time and effort into building and maintaining these unbreakable allies is a wise decision that can guide organizations toward lasting success. In the following sections, we will delve deeper into the strategies and techniques for creating and nurturing alliances that will stand the test of time.

Building and Nurturing Communication Channels with Your Allies

Let's explore the art of effective communication and discuss specific methods and tools that have proven to be particularly effective in forging unbreakable alliances. We'll also review the importance of cultivating good habits to ensure these connections remain strong and resilient.

Establishing Communication Channels

To open regular channels among your allies, understand their preferences and needs. Taking the time to learn their communication styles lets you lay a foundation for effective interactions. Also, remember to consistently apply the keys to communication: seeking thoughts and opinions, speaking in terms of people's priorities, validating them with nonjudgmental curiosity, and empowering allies with choices.

1. Conduct Open and Honest Dialogue
This is the cornerstone of any successful alliance. Establish a culture of trust and transparency by encouraging your allies to freely share their thoughts, concerns, and ideas. Reciprocate by providing the same level of openness. This creates an environment where everyone feels valued and heard, which fosters strong connections.

2. Use Multiple Communication Channels
Keep pace with the high tempo of technological communication and collaboration advancements and tools. This will require team members to be aware of and utilize the multiple channels of

communication within systems themselves, including fast advancements in AI as well as virtual reality communication. Someone will also need to be designated as the individual to keep all team members up to speed and on the same communication page.

3. Establish Clear Communication Protocols

Define expectations regarding response times, meeting frequency, and appropriate channels for different types of communication. By clarifying protocols, you create a structure that facilitates consistent and reliable communication, thus averting misunderstandings while ensuring effective collaboration.

Maintaining Communication Channels

Once communication channels are established, it is equally important to maintain and nurture them over time. This requires cultivating good habits that contribute to the longevity and strength of your alliances.

1. Consistency

Commit to regular check-ins: a weekly video call, a monthly update email, or a quarterly in-person meeting. Establishing a routine creates a sense of reliability and dependability that strengthens your alliances.

2. Active Listening

Show genuine interest in your allies' perspectives and opinions. Avoid interruptions or multitasking; instead, focus your attention solely on the person you are communicating with. Active listening deepens connections and demonstrates that you value and respect your allies' input.

3. Proactively and Regularly Provide Value

Share relevant industry insights with your allies, introduce them to potential clients or partners, or offer your expertise to help them overcome challenges. By consistently providing value, you solidify your position as a trusted ally, ensuring that your communication channels remain open and mutually beneficial.

Establishing and maintaining regular communication channels with your allies is a critical aspect of building unbreakable alliances. By embracing open and honest dialogue, using multiple communication channels, and establishing clear communication protocols, you create a strong foundation for effective communication. Additionally, cultivating good habits such as consistency, active listening, and regularly providing value will help ensure that these connections remain strong, resilient, and mutually beneficial over time.

Let's imagine a scenario where Emma, the CEO of a tech startup, wants to establish and maintain regular communication channels with her strategic partner, Logan, the CEO of a software development company. They have a shared goal of creating innovative solutions for their clients and want to ensure effective collaboration and a strong alliance.

1. Open and Honest Dialogue

Emma and Logan start their partnership by having a frank conversation about their expectations, goals, and communication preferences.

They both express their desire for transparent and frequent communication to build a strong alliance. They agree to have regular check-ins to discuss progress, challenges, and new opportunities.

2. Utilize Multiple Communication Channels

Emma and Logan leverage various channels to stay connected, including a new virtual reality interface where they can chat as if sitting in the same room together. They schedule monthly VR calls to maintain a personal connection. They also use instant messaging platforms for quick updates or questions and share project-related documents through a collaborative platform. This combination of communication channels ensures constant connectivity despite their busy schedules and distance from each other.

3. Establish Clear Communication Protocols

Emma and Logan set clear routines to streamline their interactions. They agree to respond to emails within twenty-four hours and set aside specific times for video conferences. They also outline the appropriate channels for different types of communication, such as using instant messaging for urgent matters and email for nonurgent discussions. These protocols ensure efficient and effective communication, minimizing misunderstandings.

Maintaining Communication Channels

1. Consistency

Emma and Logan commit to a monthly VR call, scheduling it on the first Friday of every month. They ensure that this meeting remains a priority and adjust their schedules accordingly. By maintaining this consistency, they create a reliable and dependable communication channel, enabling them to stay aligned and address any issues promptly.

2. Active Listening/Be Present

During their monthly VR calls, Emma and Logan practice active listening. They give each other their undivided attention, let go of personal agendas for the moment, listen carefully to each other's perspectives, and ask follow-up questions to gain a deeper understanding. By actively listening, they foster a sense of mutual respect and build a strong foundation for collaboration.

3. Regularly Provide Value

Emma regularly shares industry insights and market trends with Logan, ensuring that he is up to date with the latest developments. She also introduces him to potential clients and partners who can benefit from their joint expertise. Logan reciprocates by sharing technical knowledge and offering solutions to challenges Emma's team faces. By consistently providing value to each other, they strengthen their alliance and ensure that their communication channels remain mutually beneficial.

By implementing these techniques, Emma and Logan have success-fully established and maintained regular communication channels. Their open and honest dialogue, use of multiple communication channels, and clear communication protocols have laid the foundation for effective collaboration. Their commitment to consistency, active listening, and regularly providing value has further strengthened their alliance, ensuring that their communication channels remain strong and resilient. As a result, they can work together seamlessly, creating innovative solutions and achieving their shared goals.

Strategies for Building Trust and Credibility in Alliances over Time

Imagine a world where business alliances thrive on trust and credibility. A world where leaders understand that they can only control their own behaviors, not their allies'. In this world, the key to success lies in what we can do to deepen trust and credibility over time.

Picture yourself in a meeting, sitting across from a potential ally. You know that trust is the cornerstone of any successful partnership, and you're determined to lay a solid foundation. How do you go about it?

As you engage in conversation, you exude an aura of openness, honesty, and transparency. You understand that trust is not something that can be established overnight; it requires consistent effort and a commitment to demonstrating trustworthiness through your actions. You want your potential ally to feel safe in their decision to partner with you.

Drawing from the valuable insights shared in my previous book, *Sizing People Up*, I want to share a set of behaviors I have discovered that inspire trust and credibility in alliances over time. These behaviors are like building blocks, forming the foundation of predictability, which is the essence of trust. By consistently exhibiting these behaviors, you create an environment where trust and credibility can flourish.[1]

First and foremost, demonstrate your vested interest in your allies' success. Genuinely care about their well-being and actively support their goals. By showing that you are just as invested in their success as you are in your own, you lay the groundwork for a partnership built on mutual trust and support.[2]

Next, convey a sense of longevity in the relationship. You want your potential allies to understand that you see this partnership as an ongoing commitment. By communicating your dedication and commitment, you instill confidence in them, making them more likely to trust in your shared future.[3]

One trait you cannot overlook is reliability. Ensure that your words align with your actions, and consistently deliver on your commitments. Let your résumé speak for itself, and approach every task with energy and tenacity. Your potential ally can count on you to be dependable and trustworthy.[4]

Furthermore, actions speak louder than words. You understand the power they hold in building trust. Speak positively of others and refrain from engaging in gossip. By doing so, you create an atmosphere of trust, where your potential ally knows that you won't speak ill of them behind their back. The bridge of trust you build will span both your personal and professional interactions.[5]

Language plays a significant role in establishing trust and credibility. Communicate with clarity, empathy, positivity, and purpose in all your interactions. By using these four keys to effective communication, you ensure that your intentions and ideas are understood, which builds a sense of trust and understanding.[6]

Last, exhibit stability in times of stress and unexpected challenges. Instead of succumbing to panic or becoming overwhelmed, maintain a calm and thoughtful problem-solving approach. Your potential ally will see your ability to handle adversity with grace, further solidifying their trust in you.[7]

Building trust and credibility in alliances over time is a deliberate process that requires consistent effort and authenticity. By embodying the behaviors of vesting interest, longevity, reliability, positive actions, effective language, and stability, you pave the way for unbreakable alliances. Trust is not built overnight, but with patience, commitment, and a genuine desire to create lasting partnerships, you can foster trust and credibility that leads to shared success.

Over the course of a few months, David, a passionate and driven entrepreneur, finds himself attending various industry events in search of potential partners for his groundbreaking project. At one such event, he comes across your name and learns you are the CEO of a highly successful tech company known for its innovative solutions.

You meet up at the event and chat with David, seeking his thoughts and opinions on the industry's current challenges. Your genuine curiosity shines through as you actively listen to his ideas, recognizing the value he brings to the table. By speaking in terms of his priorities, you demonstrate that you understand his vision and are genuinely interested in helping him achieve his goals.

As time goes on, David notices a pattern in your behavior. Every time you meet, you consistently validate his thoughts and opinions, approaching his ideas with curiosity rather than judgment. This non-judgmental validation makes him feel heard and respected, building trust and credibility between you.

During one event, while discussing potential partnerships, David brings up a concern he has about the project's scalability. Instead of dismissing his concern or offering a quick solution, you empower him with choices. You present different strategies and options for over-coming scalability challenges, allowing David to make an informed decision that aligns with his vision. This empowerment leaves a lasting impression on David, reinforcing his belief in your potential as a reli-able, supportive partner.

As the months pass, you continue to cultivate trust and credibility in your interactions with David. At industry conferences and network-ing events, you consistently seek out his input, valuing his expertise and insights. You make a point to introduce him to influential individu-als within your network, showcasing your commitment to his success.

One day, amid a particularly challenging period in the industry, David calls you. He is facing unexpected hurdles that threaten to derail his project. Sensing his anxiety, you remain calm and composed, vali-dating his concerns nonjudgmentally and with curiosity. Together, you explore potential solutions, empowering David to make decisions that will help him navigate the challenging situation.

As time goes on, your partnership with David flourishes. The trust and credibility you have built over months have solidified into an unbreakable alliance. Together, you successfully launch the ground-breaking project, revolutionizing the industry and garnering attention from its leaders.

Looking back on the journey, David credits the success of the project to your consistent behavior and communication style. He appreciates the way you sought his thoughts and opinions, spoke in terms of his priorities, validated him nonjudgmentally with curiosity, and empowered him with choices. These four keys to communication have not only fostered trust and credibility but have also allowed David to thrive as a partner and leader.

In the end, the partnership between you and David becomes an inspiration to others in the industry. Your commitment to building trust and credibility over time has led to a successful project and forged a lasting alliance built on mutual respect, support, and shared success.

Using Active Curiosity to Overcome the Pitfalls of Ego in Alliances

Over my years of experience in the realm of alliances and leadership, I have witnessed a common pitfall that can hinder effective communication and engagement within these partnerships: our own egos. I find it fascinating that even the most well-intentioned individuals can fall prey to the gravitational pull of their egos, causing unnecessary challenges and obstacles within alliances.

One of the key pitfalls associated with ego is the failure to maintain a balance between self and others. As humans, we naturally have a tendency to prioritize our own needs and desires. However, in the context of alliances, recognizing the importance of collaboration and collective success is essential. When we focus excessively on our own agendas and fail to consider our allies' perspectives and needs, we create an imbalance that can strain relationships and compromise outcomes.

To overcome this pitfall, we must consciously maintain the dichotomy between self and others. We must cultivate a mindset that leans slightly toward others and recognizes the value of their contributions and perspectives. By adopting a problem-solving approach rather than a victim mentality, we can shift our focus from nursing personal grievances to finding mutually beneficial solutions. This requires a commitment to active listening, empathy, and a willingness to compromise when necessary, or what I like to call "active curiosity."

Another challenge that arises within alliances is the insidious presence of complacency. Success can sometimes breed a false sense of security, causing us to become lax in our efforts and lose sight of our sense of service. We may become disconnected from the shifting priorities and needs of our allies, leading to a breakdown in communication and engagement.

To combat complacency, we need to continuously reassess and adapt. Regular and open communication with our allies is paramount, as it allows us to stay attuned to their evolving goals and challenges. By listening to their concerns, engaging our active curiosity, and proactively offering support and expertise, we can demonstrate our commitment to the alliance's success. Additionally, regularly evaluating our own performance and seeking feedback from our allies can help us identify areas for improvement and prevent complacency from taking root. Humility is the key to being able to request and accept feedback in turn.

Last, avoid the trap of taking events or actions personally. Our egos can often cloud our judgment and interpretation of situations, leading to misunderstandings and conflicts. When we allow our ego to dictate our reactions, we risk damaging the trust and collaboration within the alliance.

To overcome this challenge, we must cultivate self-awareness and EQ. By recognizing when our ego is influencing our perspective, we can consciously choose to shift our mindset. Seeking feedback from our allies and being open to constructive criticism can help us gain a more objective view of our actions and motivations. By separating ourselves from the situation and approaching it with a level-headed perspective, we can encourage better communication and engagement within the alliance.

You can overcome the pitfalls of ego in alliances with conscious effort, self-reflection, and active curiosity. By maintaining a balance between self and others, shifting our mindset from victimhood to problem solving, avoiding complacency, and practicing self-awareness, we can create unbreakable alliances built on trust, collaboration, and shared success. The journey to overcoming ego is an ongoing one, but the rewards of effective communication and engagement within alliances are immeasurable.

Adapting and Thriving: Successful Strategies for Alliance Resilience

In a rapidly changing business landscape, the ability to adapt and evolve is crucial for the success of any alliance. To ensure this adaptability, organizations must prioritize several strategies that promote flexibility, open communication, and a collaborative mindset.

The first strategy is to reassure alliance partners with the commitment to face challenges together, free from blame, shame, and resentment. This creates a safe environment where individuals feel supported and can openly share their thoughts and concerns. By fostering a culture of psychological safety, organizations can encourage innovation and risk taking, which are essential for adaptation in a rapidly changing landscape.

Continuous communication is another key strategy for adaptability. Regular and open communication among alliance partners is crucial to staying aligned and informed about changes in the business landscape. This includes sharing market trends, technological advancements, and other relevant information. By keeping each other informed, alliance partners can collectively assess the impact of these changes and adjust their strategies accordingly.

Flexibility and agility are also essential for adaptation. Allies must be willing to embrace new ideas, experiment with different approaches, and adjust strategies and plans as needed. This requires a mindset that values learning from failure and a willingness to take calculated risks. When individuals feel safe to take risks and are not burdened by the fear of perfection, innovation can thrive, enabling alliances to adapt and evolve.

Regular joint planning sessions and reviews are another important strategy for adaptability. These sessions allow alliance partners to assess the effectiveness of their collaboration, identify areas for improvement, and adapt their strategies accordingly. Transparent communication, conducted in a respectful manner that focuses on asking "what" questions rather than "why," can facilitate constructive discussions and lead to actionable insights for adaptation.

Encouraging the exchange of knowledge and best practices among alliance partners is another effective strategy for adaptation. By sharing insights from different markets, conducting joint research, or organizing training programs for mutual learning, alliances can access a wider pool of expertise and adapt to new challenges more effectively.

Last, co-innovation and co-creation can be powerful strategies for staying ahead of the curve and adapting to changing market demands. By jointly investing in research and development, sharing resources, and collaborating on new products or services, alliances can leverage their collective strengths and create innovative solutions that meet the evolving needs of their customers.

Ultimately, adaptability is key to success in a rapidly changing business environment. By prioritizing strategies such as reassurance, continuous communication, flexibility, joint planning, shared learning, and co-innovation, allies can navigate the challenges of change and create unbreakable bonds that lead to long-term success.

There are countless businesses that exemplify unbreakable bonds that have propelled both companies to success. The size and scale of the company is irrelevant; the success lies in the execution of the alliance and the commitment that leadership had to it.

1. *Strategic Partnership Between Apple and IBM*: In 2014, Apple and IBM partnered to develop business applications for iOS devices. This alliance allowed both companies to adapt to the growing demand for mobile enterprise solutions. By combining Apple's expertise in consumer technology with IBM's knowledge in enterprise software and services, they were able to create innovative solutions that catered to businesses' changing needs.

2. *Coca-Cola and Nestlé Waters Alliance*: Coca-Cola and Nestlé Waters allied to create the joint venture called Nestlé Waters North America. This alliance enabled both companies to adapt to the increasing consumer demand for healthier beverage options. By leveraging

their combined resources, they were able to develop and market bottled water products that aligned with consumers' evolving preferences.

3. *Star Alliance*: This global airline network is another example of successful adaptation within alliances. Comprising twenty-six member airlines, Star Alliance allows passengers to seamlessly travel across different airlines within the network. This alliance has adapted to changing customer needs by offering benefits such as shared frequent-flyer programs, access to airport lounges, and coordinated flight schedules. By working together, the member airlines have adapted to evolving travel trends and provided enhanced services to their customers.

Here are a few examples of successful adaptation within alliances involving smaller companies:

1. *Collaboration Between Warby Parker and Nordstrom*: Warby Parker, an online eyewear retailer, formed a collaboration with Nordstrom, a leading fashion retailer. This alliance allowed Warby Parker to adapt to the changing retail landscape by expanding its offline presence through Nordstrom's physical stores. By leveraging Nordstrom's established retail network, Warby Parker was able to reach a wider customer base and provide a seamless, omni-channel shopping experience.

2. *Partnership Between Square and Upserve*: Square, a payment processing company, partnered with Upserve, a restaurant management platform. This alliance enabled

both companies to adapt to the evolving needs of the restaurant industry. Square integrated its payment processing solutions with Upserve's management software, providing restaurants with a comprehensive and streamlined solution for operations and payment processing. The collaboration allowed both companies to better serve their customers and adapt to the changing technology landscape.

3. *Alliance Between Patagonia and 1% for the Planet*: Patagonia, an outdoor clothing and gear company, joined forces with 1% for the Planet, a global environmental movement. This alliance enabled Patagonia to adapt to the increasing demand for sustainable and socially responsible products. Through their partnership, Patagonia committed to donating 1% of their sales to environmental causes supported by 1% for the Planet. Not only did this collaboration align with Patagonia's values, it also resonated with environmentally conscious consumers, helping the company thrive in a rapidly changing market.

These examples demonstrate how smaller companies can successfully adapt and thrive through strategic alliances. By leveraging the resources, expertise, and networks of their alliance partners, these companies were able to navigate industry shifts, reach new markets, and meet their customers' changing needs.

Addressing Concerns and Conflicts: Techniques for Effective Conflict Resolution

In the world of business alliances, conflicts and concerns are bound to arise. However, it is how we address and resolve these conflicts that truly determines the strength and longevity of the alliance. Let's explore some techniques for effective conflict resolution that can help us navigate through challenging situations while preserving our unbreakable alliances.

The first and foremost principle to keep in mind is the value of the alliance itself. By avoiding behaviors and actions that create resentment, you can prevent negative confirmation bias, distrust, and disruption from developing. However, if resentment has already taken hold, you need to have an open and honest discussion to address the underlying issues.

Encouraging open and honest communication between alliance partners is crucial. Providing a safe and respectful space for discussing concerns, conflicts, and differing perspectives allows for a deeper understanding of each other's viewpoints. Active curiosity and empathy play a significant role in fostering a constructive dialogue during these conversations.

Approaching conflicts as shared problems rather than individual issues is another effective technique for conflict resolution. By emphasizing the common goals and interests of the alliance, all parties are encouraged to work together to find mutually beneficial solutions. This collaborative problem-solving approach seeks win–win outcomes, ensuring that the resolution addresses the concerns of all parties involved.

In cases where conflicts escalate or become complex, involving a neutral third party as a mediator or facilitator can be highly beneficial. Such intermediaries can help guide the resolution process, ensure fairness, and create an environment conducive to productive discussions.

To effectively resolve conflicts, allies must focus on the underlying interests rather than rigid positions. By understanding the needs and interests of each party, it becomes easier to find creative solutions that address everyone's concerns. Encouraging alliance partners to articulate the "why" behind their positions allows for flexibility in determining the "what" and "how" of the resolution.

While aiming for consensus is ideal, it may not always be achievable. In such cases, compromise becomes essential. Encouraging each party to make concessions to reach a satisfactory resolution helps maintain a sense of fairness and ensures that no one feels unheard or ignored.

Establishing conflict resolution processes within the alliance can also be beneficial. By defining how conflicts will be addressed and resolved, everyone involved will clearly understand the steps to be taken. This clarity helps prevent misunderstandings and provides a framework for constructive conflict resolution.

Conflicts should not be seen solely as sources of problems but also as opportunities for growth and learning. Encouraging reflection and analysis of the underlying causes of conflicts allows for improved communication, decision making, and goal alignment. By learning from conflicts, the alliance can strengthen itself and become more resilient in the face of future challenges.

Regularly reviewing and evaluating the alliance's performance and dynamics is essential. By conducting these assessments, allies can identify potential concerns or conflicts early on, allowing for proactive resolution before they escalate. This approach helps maintain the health and productivity of the alliance.

Also, documenting agreements is crucial in conflict resolution. As the saying goes, "If it wasn't written down, it didn't happen." By documenting agreements, allies establish clarity and prevent future misunderstandings: all parties will be on the same page and can refer back to the agreed-upon terms if conflicts arise.

Last, allies must continuously invest in building and maintaining trust within the alliance. Trust is the foundation on which strong alliances are built. By following my five steps to trust outlined earlier in this book, alliance partners can cultivate trust and strengthen their relationships over time.

Addressing concerns and conflicts within alliances requires a proactive and constructive approach. By using the preceding techniques, partners can navigate conflicts successfully while contributing to the overall success and longevity of the alliance.

The Lessons I Learned: A Mentor's Influence on Understanding and Fulfilling Allies' Needs

As I sat down to write this section, memories of my FBI mentor and master spy recruiter, Jesse Thorn, flooded my mind. His guidance and wisdom had a profound impact on my skills of understanding and fulfilling allies' needs to create a strong value exchange. In this section, I want to share with you the valuable lessons I learned from Jesse, lessons that continue to shape my approach to building unbreakable alliances.

Jesse always stressed the importance of active curiosity. He taught me to approach every alliance with a genuine desire to discover and understand my partners' needs. It was through this curiosity that I learned to uncover their priorities, their pain points, and their unique mission and origin stories. This lesson became the compass that guided me on the path to success.

Open and transparent communication was another crucial lesson Jesse imparted. He believed that true understanding could only be achieved through meaningful conversations. I vividly remember the countless hours I spent in discussions with my alliance partners, listening intently as they shared their challenges, goals, and aspirations. Jesse taught me that by creating an environment of trust, we could unlock the true essence of their needs.

One particular story Jesse shared affected me profoundly. He recounted an experience he had with an alliance partner who seemed hesitant to voice their needs. Jesse explained how he patiently cultivated open communication and, in doing so, discovered the core challenges the partner faced. It was a transformative moment, one that solidified their bond and allowed them to align their goals. Jesse's story taught me the importance of creating a safe space for dialogue, where allies feel comfortable sharing their deepest needs and expectations.

Jesse firmly believed that setting shared goals with our alliance partners was the key to success. He compared it to standing side by side, gazing toward a common horizon. By identifying common objectives, my partners and I could create a powerful synergy that would propel us toward mutual benefits.

Another valuable lesson Jesse taught me was the art of needs assessment. He likened it to embarking on a treasure hunt, searching for the insights that would guide us to fulfill our allies' needs. Jesse showed me how surveys, interviews, and collaborative workshops could unveil invaluable insights. By proactively seeking our allies' input, we could tailor our offerings to meet their specific requirements. This personalization created value while demonstrating our unwavering commitment to their success.

Jesse often said, "To truly fulfill the needs of our allies, we must go the extra mile." He emphasized the power of customization. Whether it was customizing products, services, or support, we showed our allies that we understood their unique requirements and were dedicated to fulfilling them. Beyond creating value, this level of personalization also solidified the bonds with our allies.

Sharing resources and co-creating value was a further lesson that Jesse imparted on me. He encouraged me to identify resources, capabilities, or knowledge that I could share with my alliance partners. By providing them with valuable resources, such as market insights, technical expertise, or access to distribution channels, I contributed to their success. This sharing of resources created a true partnership, where both parties thrived.

Feedback was a compass, according to Jesse, one that guided us toward continual improvement. He urged me to regularly seek feedback from my alliance partners, to understand how well their needs were being met. By actively listening and incorporating their feedback, we both improved the value we provided and reinforced the trust and confidence our allies had in our alliance.

Last, Jesse emphasized the significance of building strong relationships with our alliance partners. He encouraged me to invest time in truly getting to know them: their organizational culture, values, and individual preferences. By forging connections through joint events, networking opportunities, or even social activities, we created bonds that withstood the test of time.

Jesse's influence on my journey has been immeasurable. Through his teachings, I learned the significance of establishing metrics and performance indicators to measure the value created for our alliance partners. It's like taking stock of the treasures we've discovered together. By tracking and measuring the impact of our contributions on their success, we could make adjustments as needed, ensuring an ongoing value exchange.

As I reflect on the lessons I learned from Jesse Thorn, I am filled with gratitude. His mentorship shaped my sense of how I can best understand and meet allies' needs. Through active curiosity, open communication, and personalization, I embraced the power of building unbreakable alliances. Jesse's teachings will forever guide me—and, I hope, you as well—on the path to success.

The Power of Expressing Appreciation and Gratitude

Appreciation and gratitude are the lifeblood of strong and resilient alliances. As leaders, it is our duty to foster an environment where these values are deeply embedded. In my time serving in the Marine Corps, I witnessed firsthand the transformative impact of expressing appreciation on the strength and longevity of our alliances.

Verbal recognition is a potent tool for conveying appreciation to our allies. Openly and sincerely acknowledging their contributions and efforts is vital. Whether in meetings, conferences, or other public forums, take the opportunity to praise their achievements and emphasize the value they bring to the alliance. However, mere generic compliments fall short. To truly convey gratitude, be specific in your recognition, demonstrating that you have attentively observed and appreciated their unique contributions. This authenticity expresses gratitude while inspiring and motivating others to continue their exceptional work.

But don't limit your appreciation to words alone. Taking the time to send personalized thank-you notes, emails, or letters adds a personal touch to expressing gratitude. Craft your message to express sincere appreciation for their specific actions or support. Delve into the details of how their contributions have boosted the alliance. Creating your own thank-you notes and stationery shows that you have invested time and thought into conveying your gratitude. Implementing a system for regularly sending these expressions ensures that your allies feel consistently valued and appreciated.

Celebrating collective achievements also strengthens the bonds within the alliance. Organize joint events, such as award ceremonies, team-building activities, or social gatherings, to commemorate and appreciate the collective accomplishments. These celebrations provide a platform to express gratitude and cultivate unity, camaraderie, and mutual respect among the allies. By tailoring these events to your team's preferences, you create an environment where allies can come together and revel in their shared success. These celebrations not only help allies express gratitude but also fortify their bonds, making them unbreakable.

Sharing success stories and case studies that highlight the positive outcomes achieved through the alliance partnership is another powerful way to express appreciation. Publicly acknowledging the role and impact of each partner showcases their invaluable contributions. Use newsletters, articles, and other platforms to disseminate these stories. By giving credit where it is due, you both express gratitude and attract potential future partners who recognize the immense value of your alliances.

To foster a culture of inclusion and appreciation, actively seek the thoughts and opinions of your allies. Make it a part of your leadership muscle memory. By integrating this practice into your daily interactions, you demonstrate that their input is genuinely valued and respected. Beyond inspiring a sense of appreciation among your allies, this inclusive approach also cultivates a shared sense of ownership within the alliance. Create opportunities for knowledge sharing and learning, where allies can contribute their expertise and gain recognition within the alliance. This further strengthens the bonds that hold you together and contributes to the unbreakable nature of your alliances.

In conclusion, expressing appreciation and gratitude is not an isolated act but an ongoing practice that you must integrate seamlessly into your leadership style. By consistently showing your gratitude to your allies, you maintain robust and healthy alliances while inspiring and motivating them to continue their exceptional work. Embrace the power of appreciation and forge unbreakable alliances that propel you toward unparalleled success.

Ten Actions

1. Schedule regular check-ins and communication sessions with longtime alliance partners to foster trust and understanding.

2. Identify reputable, established partners who align with your brand values and reputation for collaborative opportunities.

3. Establish a knowledge-sharing platform or forum within your alliance network to cultivate innovation and learning.

4. Initiate a conversation with allies to discuss expectations, goals, and communication preferences.

5. Use multiple communication channels, such as videoconferencing, virtual reality, and collaborative platforms, to stay connected.

6. Cultivate good habits like consistency, active listening, and regularly providing value to maintain strong communication channels.

7. Reach out to current allies to express genuine interest and offer support.

8. Reflect on past commitments and improve reliability to build trust and credibility.

9. Practice active curiosity and problem solving to maintain balance and avoid ego pitfalls in alliances.

10. Foster a culture of psychological safety, flexibility, and transparent communication to ensure alliance resilience and adaptation.

MASTERY

Moving Beyond Natural Talent

A man with outward courage dares to die; a
man with inner courage dares to live.
—Lao Tzu

The Journey of a Spy Recruiter

I remember when I first joined the FBI, fresh-faced and eager to make my mark. With my background in leadership from the Marine Corps and my facility for connecting with people, I was convinced that I was a natural-born recruiter of spies. I thought I had all the skills necessary to quickly and effortlessly persuade individuals to work for us.

But boy, was I in for a reality check.

In those early days, I approached my recruitment efforts with confidence and enthusiasm. I believed that my charm and persuasive abilities would be enough to convince anyone to become an asset for our agency. However, it didn't take long for me to realize that I had much to learn. I began to understand the difference between influence, persuasion, and inspiration, moving us into behavior skill mastery.

One particular case sticks out in my memory. I was tasked with recruiting an individual who had access to valuable information that could benefit our national security. I thought I had the perfect approach. Armed with all the knowledge and techniques I had acquired over the years. I was sure that I could win this person over in no time.

But as I began my conversation with them, I quickly realized that my initial approach had fallen flat. The person seemed disinterested and unimpressed by my attempts to persuade them. It was a humbling experience, to say the least. I had to reevaluate my approach and acknowledge that I still had a long way to go on my path to mastery.

Instead of giving up, I dove into a period of intense reflection and self-improvement that continues to this day. I devoured books on influence and persuasion, seeking to understand the intricacies of human behavior on a deeper level. I also sought guidance from seasoned professionals within the FBI, learning from their experiences and applying their advice to my own approach. Soon it dawned on me that mastery is a journey, not a destination.

Over time, my recruitment skills began to improve. Through countless repetitions and persistent practice, I refined my techniques and honed my ability to connect with individuals more deeply. I realized that mastery was not about innate talent alone, but about putting in the hours and consistently pushing myself to improve.

Looking back, I'm grateful for those early setbacks and humbling moments. They taught me the importance of embracing the journey and recognizing that mastery is not an endpoint, but an ongoing process. Today, I know that true mastery in recruitment, just like any other skill, comes from a combination of knowledge, experience, and the willingness to learn and grow.

So, while I may have entered the FBI with the belief that I was a natural at recruiting spies, I quickly learned that it takes many more repetitions and a commitment to continuous improvement to truly master the art of inspiration and recruitment. And that's a lesson I carry with me to this day.

Mastering behavior skills is crucial for creating and maintaining unbreakable alliances because they allow us to consciously and intentionally navigate our interactions with others. Instead of simply reacting to the world around us, we can proactively choose behaviors that benefit both ourselves and others. This level of mastery comes from a combination of knowledge and experience, often referred to as wisdom.

In his book *Chop Wood Carry Water*, Joshua Medcalf emphasizes the importance of falling in love with the process of becoming great. He highlights that greatness is not reserved for a chosen few, but rather for anyone who chooses to put in the work. This journey toward mastery is not a mistake or an accident, but a deliberate and intentional path that requires countless hours of reflection.[1]

To avoid the pain of regret later, we must push through the uncomfortable moments and stay committed to our goals and purpose. Medcalf suggests fueling our hearts with encouragement by being mindful of what we watch, read, and listen to, as well as the people we surround ourselves with. He also emphasizes the importance of positive self-talk and visualization.[2]

In the book *Pound the Stone*, Medcalf further explores the concept of mastery, particularly in the context of our early life experiences. He reminds us that greatness requires pounding the stone, by which he means putting in the hard work and effort to achieve our goals. He encourages readers to be emotionally committed to the process, but not emotionally attached to the result. This mindset allows us to stay resilient and focused on our growth, even in the face of challenges.[3]

To truly excel, we must also develop our character. Talent alone is not enough; it is character that unlocks our potential. Medcalf warns against the trap of comparison, reminding us that the grass is only greener where we water it. Instead of obsessing over our flaws, we should focus on what we have done well and how we can continue to improve. Break away from the being in the "cult of more" and having the "disease of comparison."[4]

Ultimately, the journey toward mastery is about choosing between greatness and excuses. It is about taking our talents, whether innate or developed through hard work, and elevating them to the level of mastery through repetition, reflection, refinement, and reapplication. This path requires many hours, but the rewards are worth it. By mastering behavior skills, we can create and maintain unbreakable alliances that bring success and fulfillment to our lives and the lives of those around us.

Intentional Self-Awareness in Alliance Creation

In the world of alliance creation, intentional self-awareness goes beyond being a valuable tool to be a key ingredient for achieving mastery in building strong and unbreakable alliances. By truly understanding how the world and your alliances perceive you, you gain the power to take deliberate actions that foster deeper connections and drive successful outcomes. As I often emphasize, self-awareness goes beyond mere self-knowledge; it involves actively applying that knowledge to enhance your alliance-building skills and reach a higher level of mastery.

A fundamental aspect of intentional self-awareness is the art of balancing opposing views, or dichotomies. Life is filled with dichotomies, and finding the equilibrium between them is critical for success. Take, for example, the delicate balance between humility and confidence in alliance building. The path to mastery lies in striking a harmonious blend of being humble enough to listen and learn from others, and possessing the confidence to assert your own ideas and expertise.

In his book *Think Again*, Adam Grant explores the concept of rethinking and unlearning as essential components of growth and mastery. Grant highlights the common human tendencies of confirmation bias, where we see what we want to see; and desirability bias, where we see what we expect to see. To create successful alliances, we must transcend these biases through intentional self-awareness and actively seek diverse perspectives. The purpose of learning is not merely to affirm our existing beliefs, but to evolve and expand our understanding.[5]

In the realm of intentional self-awareness, humility emerges as a crucial nutrient for the mind. Embracing the joy of being wrong and recognizing that it signifies an opportunity for growth and learning are vital aspects of being a master at creating alliances. Ideas survive not necessarily because they are true but because they are interesting. So, let go of the need to always be right and instead focus on cultivating curiosity and openness.

To excel in creating alliances, develop the skill of motivational interviewing: asking open-ended questions, listening reflectively, and affirming a person's desire and ability to change. By employing these techniques, you can create a safe and supportive environment where others feel comfortable expressing their thoughts and ideas, which in turn strengthens alliances and nurtures collaboration.[6]

Another significant aspect of intentional self-awareness in creating alliances is the ability to summarize and synthesize information effectively. By summarizing what you have heard, you enhance your understanding while laying the groundwork for meaningful change within your alliances. Summarizing well is a powerful tool for driving progress and transformation.

Furthermore, you should cultivate "inverse charisma," my term for the magnetic quality of being a great listener. By truly listening to others, we demonstrate respect, empathy, and genuine interest, which strengthens our bonds and deepens our alliances. Instead of merely consuming information, take the time to interrogate it, ask probing questions, and seek a comprehensive understanding.[7]

Last, you will need unwavering perseverance and passion, a combination often referred to as grit. As comedian Chris Rock once said, "You can be anything you're good at as long as they're hiring." By staying committed to your goals, persisting through challenges, and continually honing your skills, you can create alliances that endure and flourish.[8]

Ultimately, intentional self-awareness is a pivotal factor in mastering alliance creation. By balancing dichotomies, challenging biases, embracing humility, practicing effective communication techniques, and exhibiting perseverance and passion, you can build unbreakable alliances. So, as you embark on your journey of alliance creation, remember to engage in self-reflection; ask yourself what you have been rethinking lately; and approach the process with a growth mindset, curiosity, and openness. Through intentional self-awareness, you can elevate your alliance-building skills and achieve unparalleled success.

The Behavior Keys to Mastery

To achieve true mastery in any endeavor, you must possess four behavior keys: curiosity, humility, patience, and enthusiasm. I have found these keys essential in my own journey; when you apply them consistently, you can unlock the door to success and create unbreakable alliances along the way.

Curiosity is the fuel that drives learning and growth. It is the willingness to ask questions, explore new ideas, and seek out knowledge. Without curiosity, we become stagnant and complacent, unable to adapt to the ever-changing world around us. By cultivating a mindset of curiosity, we open ourselves up to new perspectives and possibilities, enabling us to continually evolve and improve.

Humility is the recognition that we are all lifelong learners, regardless of our accomplishments or expertise. It is the understanding that there is always more to learn and that we can benefit from others' knowledge and experiences. By approaching every situation with humility, we create an environment of collaboration and mutual respect, which fosters the development of unbreakable alliances.

Patience allows us to persevere in the face of challenges and setbacks. Mastery is not achieved overnight; it requires dedication, hard work, and a willingness to learn from failure. By cultivating patience, we are able to stay focused on our goals and maintain a long-term perspective. This resilience is what separates those who achieve mastery from those who give up at the first difficulty.

Enthusiasm is the energy that propels us forward and inspires those around us. It is the passion and excitement that we bring to our work, infecting others with a sense of purpose and motivation. By approaching every task with enthusiasm, we create an atmosphere of positivity and inspire others to join us on our journey toward mastery.

To truly embrace these behavior keys and unlock the path to mastery, adopt the mindset of an apprentice. As Robert Greene outlines in his book *Mastery*, viewing ourselves as apprentices allows us to approach every situation with a sense of curiosity and a willingness to learn. By observing those who have achieved mastery in our field, acquiring the necessary skills, and experimenting with different approaches, we can transform our mind and character, ultimately becoming the best versions of ourselves.[9]

Remember that in our quest for mastery, we are not alone; we belong to a larger universe of knowledge and experience. By embracing this interconnectedness, we can tap into the collective wisdom of others. Seeing people as they are, with a sense of humility and respect, allows us to learn from their insights and experiences, furthering our own growth and development.

The behavior keys to mastery—curiosity, humility, patience, and enthusiasm—are essential for creating unbreakable alliances and achieving success. There are no shortcuts. But by adopting the mindset of an apprentice and embracing the wisdom of others, we can use the keys to unlock our full potential and become the masters of our own destiny.

Striking the Balance: Authenticity, Boundaries, and Mastery in Alliances

While you build unbreakable alliances, authenticity and transparency will be your foundation for trust and loyalty. However, mastering the art of striking the right balance between being authentic and maintaining appropriate boundaries is essential. In this section, I reveal the intricacies of this delicate dance, focusing on both authenticity and boundaries along with the theme of mastery.

To create authentic alliances with clear boundaries, regular self-assessment is crucial. We must constantly evaluate how our behavior makes us feel and its impact on others. This introspection allows us to identify any signs of resentment, unhealthy behaviors, or compromised authenticity. By acknowledging and addressing these negative emotions, we can strive for personal mastery and ensure our actions align with our core values and beliefs.

Simultaneously, calibrating the impact of our behavior on others requires a deep understanding of their comfort levels. Establishing a comfort baseline with allies and assessing the effects of actions over time are crucial steps. This level of mastery demands a heightened sense of EQ and empathy. It involves recognizing and respecting others' unique boundaries and comfort zones while remaining true to ourselves.

Mastering the sweet spot where authenticity aligns with others' boundaries and comfort levels is vital for forming unbreakable alliances. It requires a delicate balance between self-awareness, empathy, and adaptability. Mastery in this realm is not about hiding or pretending to be someone else, but rather about understanding and respecting others' boundaries while expressing our true selves.

To further develop mastery in navigating these dynamics, open and honest communication becomes paramount. Transparently sharing intentions, beliefs, and values with allies fosters trust and strengthens alliances. Mastery lies in the ability to convey authenticity while also respecting others' boundaries. It involves actively listening to allies' feedback and cues, understanding when boundaries may be crossed, and making the necessary adjustments.

The journey toward mastering authenticity, boundaries, and alliances is an ongoing process. It requires dedication, self-reflection, and a commitment to personal growth. By actively seeking feedback, learning from experiences, and adapting our behaviors, we can refine our approach and elevate their mastery.

Mastering the right blend of authenticity and boundaries that builds unbreakable alliances involves constant self-assessment, understanding the impact of our behavior on others, and respecting their comfort zones. We must strive for open communication, listen actively, and commit to personal growth. By perfecting this balance, we can cultivate alliances rooted in trust, loyalty, and unwavering support.

Self-Mastery for Alliance Creation

In my own humble pursuit of excellence in alliance creation, I have come to realize that self-mastery is the foundation for achieving exceptional results. Joe Navarro's book *Be Exceptional* offers invaluable insights into the importance of self-mastery and provides practical strategies for individuals seeking to become masters in alliance creation.[10]

Navarro emphasizes that self-mastery is at the heart of what makes exceptional people exceptional. It involves investing in our own knowledge growth and potential through self-apprenticeship. As aspiring masters in alliance creation, we must take full responsibility for our own improvement and actively seek opportunities for growth. To do so, we may need to invest in personal development resources, attend workshops or seminars, or seek guidance from mentors and guides who can provide valuable insights and guidance.[11]

One key aspect of self-mastery is the concept of self-apprenticeship. Navarro emphasizes that truly exceptional individuals not only seek to lead, but also strive to be worthy of leading. This means constantly working on ourselves and our skills, continuously improving and growing. By carving out time to work on ourselves throughout our lives, we can develop the necessary qualities and expertise to become exceptional leaders in alliance creation.[12]

Creating a self-apprenticeship library is a powerful tool for continuous learning and self-mastery. Choose resources that align with your goals and areas of interest in alliance creation. Include books, articles, podcasts, or online courses that provide valuable insights and knowledge. By immersing ourselves in these resources, we can expand our understanding and gain the necessary expertise to create unbreakable alliances.

Striking a balance between self-mentorship and seeking out guides will aid us in honing our self-mastery. While self-mentorship allows us to take ownership of our growth and development, seeking guidance from experienced mentors and guides can provide us with valuable perspectives and insights. The key is to recognize and embrace both forms of acquiring knowledge and wisdom while finding the proportion of each that works best for our personal journey toward mastery.[13]

Emotional balance is another critical aspect of self-mastery. To create unbreakable alliances, we must first master our own emotions. Navarro advises us to look for strategies to mitigate stress and avoid emotional hijacking, as these can hinder our ability to make sound decisions and build strong relationships. By mastering our emotions, we can approach challenges with stability and clarity, fostering trust and rapport with our allies.[14]

Conscientiousness is a key trait of exceptional individuals. Navarro highlights the importance of accomplishing tasks while considering their impact on others. As aspiring masters in alliance creation, we must reflect on how we want to be known and act powerfully in alignment with our values and goals. By identifying and addressing our own weaknesses, and performing even the smallest tasks with diligence, we can develop habits for discipline and create a life of excellence.[15]

Time management is crucial for self-mastery. Exceptional individuals understand the value of time and the importance of making the most of each moment. By creating a daily plan and utilizing tools such as 3×5 cards, we can optimize our productivity and unlock our talents through deliberate practice. Consistently managing our time well allows us to keep improving while progressing toward mastery in alliance creation.[16]

Perseverance is a characteristic shared by all masters. We must embrace the mindset that success is a result of hard work and dedication, and we must never give up on our goals, even in the face of challenges and setbacks. Perseverance fuels our growth and development, allowing us to overcome obstacles and achieve exceptional results in alliance creation.

Self-mastery is the cornerstone of achieving excellence in alliance creation. By investing in our own growth and potential through self-apprenticeship, striking a balance between self-mentorship and external guidance, mastering our emotions, practicing conscientiousness, managing our time effectively, and persevering through challenges, we can become masters in creating unbreakable allies, and in turn achieve exceptional results in our personal and professional lives.

Guiding Principles for Long-Term Success

To end this chapter on mastery, I want to leave you with some final thoughts and advice for mastering behavior skills and creating unbreakable alliances for long-term success. These guiding principles, when implemented consistently and with purpose, will pave the way for a prosperous life and career.

1. Practice Humility and Confidence—the Dynamic Duo

Mastery of behavior skills begins with embracing the delicate balance between humility and confidence. Humility allows us to acknowledge our limitations, biases, and the vast knowledge that others possess. It enables empathy, deep listening, and a genuine desire to understand and learn from others. Confidence, on the other hand, is rooted in self-awareness, a belief in our own abilities, and a solid understanding of our strengths. It inspires trust and respect in our allies and enables us to effectively navigate the challenges that come our way. By cultivating both humility and confidence, you will create a powerful presence that draws others toward you and strengthens your alliances.

2. Get in Your Reps: The Power of Practice

Becoming a master of behavior skills requires dedicated practice. It is not enough just to understand the concepts intellectually; you must consistently apply them in your everyday interactions. Just as an athlete trains their body to perform at its best, you must train your mind and behavior skills through repetition. Seek out opportunities to engage in conversations, negotiations, and relationship-building exercises. With each repetition, you strengthen the neural pathways in your brain, allowing you to respond instinctively and skillfully in any situation. The more you practice, the more refined and natural your behavior skills will become.

3. Stay Curious to Fuel Your Growth

A truly masterful individual never stops learning. Cultivate an insatiable curiosity about human behavior, psychology, and the intricacies of building strong alliances. Stay up to date on the latest research, seek out new perspectives, and challenge your own assumptions. By remaining curious, you open yourself up to new possibilities and gain a deeper understanding of others. Curiosity also fuels your ability to ask insightful questions, uncover hidden motivations, and adapt your behavior to different individuals and contexts. Embrace a continuous-learning mindset, and let curiosity be the compass that guides your journey toward mastery.

4. Place Value on Healthy Allies Above All Else

In the pursuit of success, it can be tempting to prioritize quantity over quality when it comes to alliances. However, true mastery lies in placing value on healthy and mutually beneficial relationships. Seek out allies who genuinely care about your growth and well-being, and reciprocate that care. These allies will support you in times of triumph and challenge and uplift you during moments of adversity. Surround yourself with individuals who inspire you to be your best self, and together, you will forge unbreakable alliances that propel you toward long-term success.

The journey toward mastering behavior skills and creating unbreakable alliances lasts a lifetime. It requires humility, confidence, consistent practice, a curious mindset, and cultivating healthy alliances. By embracing these principles, you will unlock the keys to long-term success in your personal and professional lives. So, go forth with determination, passion, and a commitment to growth, and watch as your mastery transforms your life and propels you toward greatness.

Conclusion

As I sat across from my mentor, Jesse Thorne, a seasoned FBI agent with decades of experience, I couldn't help but feel a sense of awe and gratitude. We had just wrapped up a successful joint operation with the CIA and the British, a mission that required the utmost collaboration and trust between our agencies. It was a testament to the power of long-term alliances.

Reflecting on the journey that had led me here, I realized the importance of maintaining and growing alliances throughout my career as a spy recruiter. It wasn't just about the immediate objectives or the thrill of the chase; it was about building unbreakable bonds based on shared goals and unwavering support.

One lesson that Jesse imparted to me early on was the value of expressing appreciation and gratitude to our allies. He believed that gratitude was the greatest gift we could give, a way to acknowledge the trust and commitment that had been forged through our alliances. And he was right.

Over the years, I learned that maintaining and growing alliances required intentional effort. It wasn't enough to simply establish communication channels or build trust; it required consistent check-ins, open dialogue, and a willingness to adapt and address conflicts head on. It meant prioritizing the needs and interests of our allies, even when it meant putting our own agenda aside.

But perhaps the most important lesson I learned was the journey of mastering behavior skills. Mastery wasn't about natural talent or innate abilities; it was about intentional self-awareness and the commitment to continuous growth. It meant embracing curiosity, humility, patience, and enthusiasm as the keys to unlocking our full potential.

As you embark on your own journey to mastery and the creation of unbreakable alliances, remember that success lies in the strategies and techniques outlined in this book, as well as your commitment to embodying these principles in your everyday interactions. Trust the process, embrace the challenges, and never underestimate the power of a strong alliance. Together, you and your allies can achieve mastery.

MASTERY EXERCISES

Never regret your past. Rather, embrace it as the teacher that it is.
—Robin Sharma

Taking Your Mastery to the Next Level: Practical Exercises

In this chapter section, we will explore practical exercises that will help deepen your understanding and mastery of the behaviors needed for creating unbreakable allies. These exercises are designed to support the concepts discussed in each chapter of this book. By engaging in these exercises, you will be able to put into practice the strategies and techniques presented, allowing you to truly internalize and embody the principles of alliance building.

To get the most out of these exercises, I suggest that you reread the chapter, take time to reflect on the concepts, and make notes of any insights or questions that arise. This reflective process will help you identify areas where you can improve and areas where you excel.

As you've seen, most chapters ended with a list of ten actions that summarized the key takeaways and served as a guide for implementing the principles discussed in the chapter. It is important to go through each action in the lists and consider how you can incorporate it into your daily interactions.

Once you have completed the reflective and note-taking process, it is time to tackle the practical mastery exercises that follow. The exercises are grouped according to the chapter they support, four per chapter. Each exercise is designed to provide you with an opportunity to practice and refine your alliance-building skills.

When approaching these exercises, it is essential to take them one at a time. Begin by reflecting on the exercise and strategizing how you can implement it in your professional and personal lives. Consider the potential challenges you may face and think about how you can overcome them.

After strategizing, give the exercise a try. Engage in real-life scenarios or simulations that let you put the exercise into action. Be mindful of the outcomes and reflect on the results. Did the exercise yield the desired outcome? If not, make adjustments and try again. Remember, mastery is a process, one requiring perseverance and a willingness to learn from both successes and failures.

This cycle will set you on the path of falling in love with the process, rather than focusing solely on the destination. As Joshua Medcalf advised in his image of pounding a stone, each repetition and adjustment will further hone your ability to build unbreakable alliances.

So, get ready to embark on this journey of self-improvement and skill development. Take the time to engage in these practical exercises, and watch your ability to create unbreakable allies flourish.

Remember, true mastery comes from consistent effort, so commit to the process, and let's start pounding the stone together.

Mastery Exercises

Chapter 1: FOCUS

Exercise 1: Reflect on the Importance of Alliances
- Take a few moments to think about your personal and professional goals and how alliances could contribute to successfully achieving them.
- Write down three specific examples of how alliances have improved your life.
- Share your examples with a partner or a trusted friend and discuss how these alliances have influenced your overall well-being.

Exercise 2: Build Trust and Demonstrate Trustworthiness
- Identify three behaviors of trust that you value the most in your relationships.
- Reflect on your own actions and behaviors and assess how well you demonstrate these behaviors of trust.
- Choose one behavior that you would like to improve on and create an action plan to practice it consistently in your interactions with others.
- Seek feedback from someone you trust to evaluate your progress and make adjustments if necessary.

Exercise 3: Prioritize the Needs of Others

- Choose a person in your life (either personal or professional) whose needs you would like to prioritize.
- Take some time to understand their goals, needs, and interests by having a conversation with them or, if needed, researching them.
- Reflect on how you can support and contribute to their success, and create a plan to take specific actions to meet their needs.
- Track your progress and evaluate the impact of prioritizing their needs on building trust and goodwill in your relationship.

Exercise 4: Enhance Communication for Building Alliances

- Practice active listening by choosing a conversation with someone in which to focus on fully understanding their perspective without interrupting or making judgments.
- Tailor your communication to someone's priorities by identifying their preferred communication style and adjusting your approach accordingly.
- Engage in nonjudgmental curiosity by asking open-ended questions and seeking to understand their thoughts and feelings.
- Empower others with choices by providing them with options and involving them in decision-making processes.
- Reflect on the outcomes of your enhanced communication techniques and how they have contributed to building unbreakable alliances.

Chapter 2: TRUST

Exercise 1: Build Rapport and Trust

- Choose a person in either your personal or professional life with whom you would like to build rapport and trust.
- Reflect on your interactions with this person and identify any behaviors or actions that may be hindering the development of trust.
- Create a plan to prioritize building rapport and trust in your interactions with them, focusing on actions such as active listening, empathy, and authenticity.
- Track your progress and evaluate the impact of your efforts on strengthening the relationship and fostering trust.

Exercise 2: Shift Your Mindset to Understanding and Connection

- Take some time to reflect on your mindset toward others, particularly in situations where you may feel the urge to control or manipulate.
- Identify any underlying fears or insecurities that may be driving this mindset and explore ways to address and overcome them.
- Shift your focus to understand and connect with others by practicing empathy, listening actively, and seeking to find common ground.
- Reflect on the impact of this mindset shift on your interactions and relationships, both personal and professional.

Exercise 3: Commit to Integrity in Leadership

- Consider your leadership approach and assess whether you have been employing any manipulative strategies or actions.
- Commit to acting with integrity in your leadership role and identify specific strategies or behaviors that align with this commitment.
- Seek feedback from colleagues or trusted individuals to assess your progress in upholding integrity in your leadership approach.
- Reflect on your leadership style and refine it continuously to ensure it aligns with your commitment to authenticity and trust building.

Exercise 4: Practice Active Listening and Understanding Perspectives

- Choose a conversation or interaction with someone where active listening and understanding their perspective is crucial.
- Practice giving the person your full attention by eliminating distractions and focusing on their words and body language.
- Ask open-ended questions to encourage them to share more and gain a deeper understanding of their thoughts and feelings.
- Reflect on the impact of your understanding and active listening on the quality of the conversation and the level of trust and connection established.

Chapter 3: COMMUNICATE

Exercise 1: Practice Active Listening and Adaptation

- Choose a conversation or interaction with someone and practice active listening by giving your full attention and showing genuine interest in their thoughts and opinions.
- Reflect on their communication preferences and adapt your delivery style to match their needs.
- Ask the person afterward to provide feedback on how well you listened and adapted, and whether they felt understood and valued in the conversation.

Exercise 2: Express Empathy and Validation

- Choose a person in your life with whom you would like to strengthen your relationship and build trust.
- Practice active listening and empathize with their experiences and emotions, validating their thoughts and feelings without judgment.
- Engage in a conversation where you actively show empathy and validate their perspective, focusing on understanding rather than providing solutions.
- Reflect on the impact of your empathy and validation on the relationship- and trust-building process.

Exercise 3: Encourage Active Participation

- Choose a group setting or team meeting where you can practice encouraging active participation.
- Create a safe and supportive environment by inviting others to share their ideas and opinions.

- Help others take ownership of their actions by offering guidance and support in their decision-making process.
- Reflect on the level of engagement and participation in the group, as well as the quality of the ideas and decisions generated.

Exercise 4: Practice Empathy in Understanding Perspectives

- Select a person or situation where understanding their motivations and needs is crucial.
- Practice active listening while seeking to understand their unique context in order to empathize with them.
- Consider their perspective and needs when engaging with them, adjusting your approach to convey your empathy.
- Reflect on the impact of your empathy in understanding their perspective and fostering a stronger connection.

Chapter 4: INSPIRE

Exercise 1: Inspire Others Through Solutions

- Choose a person in your life or in a professional setting where you would like to inspire others.
- Shift your focus from yourself to the other person and actively listen to their needs and challenges.
- Offer solutions that specifically address their needs and aspirations and show genuine interest in their success.
- Reflect on the impact of your approach to inspiring and motivating the other person.

Exercise 2: Inspire Others Genuinely, Without Manipulation

- Reflect on your current approach to inspiring others and assess if you are unintentionally employing any manipulative tactics.
- Prioritize the genuine inspiration that comes from within the other person, focusing on understanding their intrinsic motivators.
- Seek feedback from others to evaluate the authenticity and effectiveness of your approach.
- Continuously reflect upon and adjust your methods to ensure they align with genuine inspiration and trust building.

Exercise 3: Build Trust and Communicate Effectively

- Choose a relationship or alliance where trust and effective communication are important.
- Reflect on your current communication patterns and identify any areas for improvement in building trust.
- Practice active listening and empathy to better understand the priorities and challenges of your ally.
- Experiment with different communication techniques that prioritize trust and collaboration.
- Reflect on how your improved communication has strengthened and deepened the alliance.

Exercise 4: Discover Allies' Priorities and Challenges

- Select a person or team with whom you have an alliance.
- Practice active listening and empathy to discover their priorities and challenges.

- Engage in conversations that allow them to openly share their goals and aspirations.
- Use this information to tailor your communication and actions to create a stronger connection and collaboration.

Chapter 5: OWN IT

Exercise 1: Prioritize Relationships and Trust in Conflicts

- Identify a conflict situation where maintaining the relationship and trust is crucial.
- List the potential material outcomes on which you may need to compromise to prioritize the relationship.
- Practice letting go of certain outcomes if necessary and focus on finding a mutually acceptable solution.
- Reflect on the impact of prioritizing relationships and trust in the resolution of the conflict.

Exercise 2: Understand Others' Perspectives in Conflicts

- Choose a conflict situation where understanding the context and perspective of others is important.
- Engage in thoughtful conversations with the individuals involved and ask open-ended questions to gain deeper insights.
- Practice active listening and empathy to truly understand their viewpoint and feelings.
- Reflect on how this understanding has influenced your approach to conflict resolution.

Exercise 3: Take Ownership of Behavior in Conflicts

- Reflect on a conflict situation where your actions may have made the other person feel unsafe or unheard.
- Take ownership of your behavior and actions, acknowledging any mistakes or negative impact.
- Adjust your approach and communication style to ensure a safe and respectful environment.
- Reflect on the impact of taking ownership and adjusting your behavior in conflict resolution.

Exercise 4: Practice Active Listening and Empathetic Communication in Conflicts

- Choose a conflict situation where active listening and empathetic communication are important.
- Practice active listening by giving the other person your full attention and seeking to understand their viewpoint.
- Engage in empathetic communication by validating their feelings and finding common ground.
- Reflect on the impact of active listening and empathetic communication in resolving the conflict and building a stronger relationship.

Chapter 6: CONTEXT

Exercise 1: Listen Actively to Understand Perspectives

- Choose a conversation or interaction where you can practice active listening.

- Take the time to fully engage and listen to the other person, and seek to understand their unique perspective and experiences.
- Avoid interrupting the person or making assumptions, and instead focus on truly understanding their viewpoint.
- Reflect on how actively listening and understanding others' perspectives enhances your communication and relationships.

Exercise 2: Show Empathy and Respect in Engagement

- Select a situation or discussion where you can practice empathy and respect.
- Engage with others by giving their ideas fair consideration, even if they differ from your own.
- Practice empathy by putting yourself in their shoes and seeking to understand their reasoning and emotions.
- Reflect on the impact of approaching interactions with empathy and respect on fostering positive relationships and productive conversations.

Exercise 3: Cultivate a Cosmic Perspective

- Dedicate time to seeking knowledge and understanding nature's behavior through research, reading, or exploration.
- Embrace a mindset of exploration and discovery, allowing yourself to see the bigger picture and think beyond your immediate surroundings.
- Reflect on how cultivating a cosmic perspective influences your thinking and decision making in both personal and professional contexts.

Exercise 4: Collaborate with People Who Have Different Skill Sets

- Identify a colleague or professional contact whose skill set or expertise differs from your own.
- Reach out to them and propose a collaborative project or partnership that leverages each other's strengths.
- Embrace the opportunity to learn from each other and create a synergy that enhances the outcome.
- Reflect on the benefits and challenges of collaborating with someone who brings different skills and perspectives to the table.

Chapter 7: BUILD

Exercise 1: Check in Regularly for Trust and Understanding

- Schedule regular check-ins and communication sessions with your long-term alliance partners.
- Use these sessions to foster trust and understanding by openly discussing challenges, goals, and expectations.
- Practice active listening and empathy during these check-ins to deepen your understanding of each other's perspectives.
- Reflect on how regular communication contributes to building trust and maintaining a strong alliance.

Exercise 2: Identify Reputable Partners for Collaboration

- Conduct research to identify reputable and established partners who align with your brand values and reputation.
- Seek out collaborative opportunities with these partners to leverage their expertise and enhance your offerings.

- Prioritize due diligence and ensure alignment in goals, values, and approaches before entering into a partnership.
- Reflect on the benefits and challenges of collaborating with reputable partners and the impact it has on your brand.

Exercise 3: Establish a Knowledge-Sharing Platform

- Create a knowledge-sharing platform or forum within your alliance network.
- Encourage members to share innovative ideas, best practices, and lessons learned.
- Foster a culture of collaboration and continuous learning within the alliance.
- Reflect on the impact of the knowledge-sharing platform on cultivating innovation and growth within the alliance network.

Exercise 4: Discuss Expectations and Communication Preferences

- Start a conversation with your allies to openly discuss expectations, goals, and communication preferences.
- Seek alignment and understanding to ensure effective communication and collaboration.
- Practice active listening and empathy during these conversations to develop a deeper connection.
- Reflect on how openly discussing expectations and preferences strengthens alliances.

ACKNOWLEDGMENTS

I extend my deepest appreciation to the teachers, mentors, and dear friends from my time at the FBI, who have continuously inspired and guided me. John Sapanara, Joe Navarro, and Jack Schafer, your knowledge, expertise, and unwavering support have been instrumental in shaping my understanding and perspective. Thank you for your guidance and friendship.

To the guests and followers of my Forged by Trust podcast, my fellow Marines, my Naval Academy classmates, and even my high school classmates, I am truly thankful for the camaraderie and support you have shown me throughout the years.

A special acknowledgment goes to my agent, Nathaniel Jacks from Inkwell Management. Nathaniel, your professionalism and friendship have been invaluable, and I am grateful for your unwavering belief in my work. I also want to express my gratitude to the incredible team at Matt Holt/BenBella Books, who have skillfully crafted this book into something extraordinary.

To my beloved wife, Kim, and my amazing adult children, Kevin and Katelyn, you are my pillars of strength and my greatest sources of inspiration. Your unwavering support, encouragement, and understanding have been instrumental in bringing this book to life. I am forever grateful for your love and belief in me.

And lastly, to you, the reader. It is with heartfelt appreciation that I acknowledge our connection. I am deeply grateful that our paths have crossed, and I hope that the pages of this book have ignited a spark within you. May the wisdom and insights shared here positively impact all the relationships in your life, and may you find inspiration on your own unique journey.

With warmest regards and heartfelt thanks,

Robin

NOTES

Chapter 1—Focus

1   Brené Brown, *Braving the Wonderness* (New York: Random House, 2019), 63–88.
2   Simon Sinek, *The Infinite Game* (New York: Portfolio, 2019), 103–130.

Chapter 2—Trust

1   Robin Dreeke, *It's Not All About "Me": The Top Ten Techniques for Quick Rapport with Anyone* (Fredericksburg, VA: People Formula, 2011).
2   Dreeke, *It's Not All About "Me."*
3   Tasha Eurich, *Insight: The Surprising Truth About How Others See Us, How We See Ourselves, and Why the Answers Matter More Than We Think* (New York: Penguin Random House, 2017), 127–156.
4   Eurich, *Insight*; Simon Sinek, *Leaders Eat Last: Why Some Teams Pull Together and Others Don't* (New York: Portfolio, 2017).
5   Robin Dreeke, "Mark Bowden," February 23, 2023, in *Forged by Trust*, podcast, 50:59, https://www.peopleformula.com/forged-by-trust-podcast.
6   Robin Dreeke, *Sizing People Up: A Veteran FBI Agent's User Manual for Behavior Prediction* (New York: Portfolio, 2020), 101–102.

Chapter 3—Communicate

1   Ryan Holiday, *Lives of the Stoics* (New York: Profile, 2022).
2   William Moulton Marston, *Emotions of Normal People* (Scottsdale, AZ: Target Training International, 2012).

3   Daniel Goleman, *Emotional Intelligence: Why It Can Matter More Than IQ* (New York: Bantam, 1995).

4   Jack Schafer and Marvin Karlins, *The Like Switch: An Ex-FBI Agent's Guide to Influencing, Attracting, and Winning People Over* (New York: Atria, 2015); Jack Schafer and Marvin Karlins, *The Truth Detector: An Ex-FBI Agent's Guide for Getting People to Reveal the Truth* (New York: Atria, 2020).

Chapter 4—Inspire

1   *Merriam-Webster*, s.v. "influence (*n.*)," accessed August 25, 2023, https://www.merriam-webster.com/dictionary/influence#dictionary-entry-1.

2   Neil deGrasse Tyson, *Starry Messenger: Cosmic Perspectives on Civilization* (New York: Henry Holt, 2022); Walter Isaacson, *Einstein: The Man, the Genius, and the Theory of Relativity* (New York: Simon & Schuster, 2007).

3   Randy Olson, *The Narrative Gym: Introducing the ABT Framework for Messaging and Communication* (Middletown, DE: Prairie Starfish Press, 2020).

Chapter 5—Own It

1   Ryan Holiday, *Ego Is the Enemy* (New York: Portfolio, 2016).

2   Holiday, *Ego Is the Enemy*.

3   Holiday, *Ego Is the Enemy*.

4   Robin Sharma, *The Monk Who Sold His Ferrari* (Toronto: HarperSanFrancisco, 1997).

5   Sharma, *The Monk Who Sold His Ferrari*, 93–143.

6   Sharma, *The Monk Who Sold His Ferrari*, 72–92.

7   Sharma, *The Monk Who Sold His Ferrari*.

8   Sharma, *The Monk Who Sold His Ferrari*.

9   Sharma, *The Monk Who Sold His Ferrari*, 32–40.

10   Ryan Holiday, *Stillness Is the Key* (New York: Portfolio, 2019).

11   Robert Greene, *The Laws of Human Nature* (New York: Penguin, 2019).

12   Greene, *The Laws of Human Nature*, 28–35.

13   Greene, *The Laws of Human Nature*, 13–41.

14   Greene, *The Laws of Human Nature*, 13–41.

15   Jack Schafer and Marvin Karlins, *The Truth Detector: An Ex-FBI Agent's Guide for Getting People to Reveal the Truth* (New York: Atria, 2020).

16   Schafer and Karlins, *The Truth Detector*, 22–54.

17   Schafer and Karlins, *The Truth Detector*, 118–153.

18   Ryan Holiday, *Discipline Is Destiny* (New York: Portfolio, 2022).

19   Holiday, *Discipline Is Destiny*.

20   Holiday, *Discipline Is Destiny*.

Chapter 6—Context

1   Neil deGrasse Tyson, *Starry Messenger: Cosmic Perspectives on Civilization* (New York: Henry Holt, 2022).

2   Walter Isaacson, *Leonardo da Vinci* (New York: Simon & Schuster, 2017).

3   Eckhart Tolle, *The Power of Now* (Mumbai: Yogi Impressions LLP, 2001).

4   Tolle, *The Power of Now*.

5   Jocko Willink and Leif Babin, *The Dichotomy of Leadership* (New York: St. Martin's Press, 2018).

6   Willink and Babin, *The Dichotomy of Leadership*, 15–36.

7   Willink and Babin, *The Dichotomy of Leadership*, 83–106.

8   Willink and Babin, *The Dichotomy of Leadership*.

9   Diane Hamilton, *Cracking the Curiosity Code* (Columbus, OH: Gatekeeper Press, 2018).

10   Hamilton, *Cracking the Curiosity Code*.

11   Hamilton, *Cracking the Curiosity Code*, 42–53.

12   Simon Sinek, *Start with Why: How Great Leaders Inspire Everyone to Take Action* (New York: Portfolio, 2009), 1–7.

13   Sinek, *Start with Why*, 90–92.

14   Simon Sinek, *Leaders Eat Last: Why Some Teams Pull Together and Others Don't* (New York: Portfolio, 2017), 23–30.

15   Reed Hastings and Erin Meyer, *No Rules Rules: Netflix and the Culture of Reinvention* (New York: Penguin, 2020), 3–18.

16   Hastings and Meyer, *No Rules Rules*, 26–31.

Chapter 7—Build

1   Robin Dreeke, *Sizing People Up: A Veteran FBI Agent's User Manual for Behavior Prediction* (New York: Portfolio, 2020).

2   Dreeke, *Sizing People Up*, 49–82.

3   Dreeke, *Sizing People Up*, 83–115.

4   Dreeke, *Sizing People Up*, 115–144.

5   Dreeke, *Sizing People Up*, 145–168.

6   Dreeke, *Sizing People Up*, 169–196.

7   Dreeke, *Sizing People Up*, 197–236.

Chapter 8—Mastery

1   Joshua Medcalf, *Chop Wood Carry Water: How to Fall in Love with the Process of Becoming Great* (self-pub., CreateSpace, 2015).

2   Medcalf, *Chop Wood Carry Water*, 26–30.

3   Joshua Medcalf, *Pound the Stone: 7 Lessons to Develop Grit on the Path to Mastery* (self-pub., Train to Be Clutch, 2017).

4   Medcalf, *Pound the Stone*.

5   Adam Grant, *Think Again: The Power of Knowing What You Don't Know* (New York: Viking, 2021).

6   Grant, *Think Again*, 146–151.

7   Grant, *Think Again*, 143–159.

8   Grant, *Think Again*, 230.

9   Robert Greene, *Mastery* (New York: Penguin, 2012).

10 Joe Navarro, *Be Exceptional: Master the Five Traits That Set Extraordinary People Apart* (New York: William Morrow, 2021).

11 Navarro, *Be Exceptional*.

12 Navarro, *Be Exceptional*, 5–70.

13 Navarro, *Be Exceptional*, 5–70.

14 Navarro, *Be Exceptional*, 39–47.

15 Navarro, *Be Exceptional*, 33–36.

16 Navarro, *Be Exceptional*, 50, 129.

INDEX

ABOUT THE AUTHOR

Robin Dreeke, a distinguished author and retired FBI agent, is widely recognized for his expertise in the field of counterintelligence and behavioral analysis. With an illustrious career that includes serving as the Chief of the Counterintelligence Division's Behavioral Analysis Program, Robin has dedicated his life to understanding human behavior and its impact on security and intelligence operations.

Drawing upon his extensive experience and deep understanding of human psychology, Robin has authored numerous groundbreaking works that have garnered critical acclaim. His books delve into the intricacies of interpersonal communication, trust-building, and the art of influence, providing invaluable insights for professionals in fields such as law enforcement, intelligence, and business.

Robin's exceptional ability to decode human behavior and uncover hidden motivations has made him a sought-after speaker and consultant, both nationally and internationally. His captivating presentations and engaging workshops have empowered countless individuals and organizations to enhance their communication skills, build strong relationships, and navigate complex social dynamics.

With a unique blend of expertise, practical knowledge, and a genuine passion for helping others, Robin Dreeke continues to be a leading authority in the field of behavioral analysis.

Ignite Your Audience with Robin's Inspiring Keynotes!

Robin's keynotes delve deep into the art of building Unbreakable Alliances and fostering Trust. Drawing from his extensive experience in the field of human behavior, he shares practical strategies and actionable techniques to help individuals and organizations create unbreakable alliances.

Book Robin for your event:

robindreeke.com/contact

Learn from the Master: Robin's "Keys to Communication" Video Series on YouTube

Enhance your communication skills with Robin's exclusive YouTube video series. Join him as he teaches you the critical Keys to Effective Communication you just learned about. These valuable techniques and real-life examples will empower you to navigate any social or professional situation with confidence.

robindreeke.com/courses

Visit Robin's Website

For more resources, including additional behavior videos, books, and information about Robin's speaking engagements, visit his website at https://robindreeke.com. Discover a wealth of knowledge and take the first step toward building Unbreakable Alliances, forged on a foundation of Trust.

robindreeke.com